MORE

SENSATIONAL
KNITTED
SOCKS

Charlene Schurch

Martingale®
& COMPANY

DEDICATION

For Fred

ACKNOWLEDGMENTS

A very special thank-you to Martingale & Company's talented and knowledgeable staff. Special thanks go to Ursula Reikes, my editor, who has made the complicated accessible. Thanks also to Mary Green for her confidence in socks. Additionally, I'd like to thank my friends and members of Yahoo Sockknitters for test knitting the patterns: Carol Breitner, Carol Davis, Donna Downey, Sue Flynn, Shannidy Hough, Janice Hopper, John Jarvis, Elaine McRee, Beth Parrott, Joan Tilston, Bonnie Welch, and Grace Wohlfart.

Thanks also go to all the yarn companies who so generously provided the yarn. There are so many wonderful yarns for knitting socks these days. They include: Lang Jawoll from Berroco, Tuffy and Durasport from Briggs and Little, Baby Ull from Dale of Norway, Essential from Knit Picks, Sock! from Lisa Souza, Shepherd Sport and Shepherd Worsted from Lorna's Laces, Gems Merino Opal from Louet Sales, Bearfoot and Weaver's Wool Quarters from Mountain Colors, Lola from Schaefer Yarn, fingering-weight yarn from Strickwear.com, Frog Tree Alpaca from T & C Imports, South Down sock yarn from Twist of Fate Spinnery, and Lana Grossa Meilenweit from Unicorn.

CREDITS

CEO ▪ Tom Wierzbicki

Publisher ▪ Jane Hamada

Editorial Director ▪ Mary V. Green

Managing Editor ▪ Tina Cook

Technical Editor ▪ Ursula Reikes

Copy Editor ▪ Liz McGehee

Design Director ▪ Stan Green

Illustrator ▪ Robin Strobel

Cover and Text Designer ▪ Shelly Garrison

Photographer ▪ Brent Kane

More Sensational Knitted Socks
© 2007 by Charlene Schurch

Martingale®
& COMPANY

That Patchwork Place®

Martingale & Company
20205 144th Ave. NE
Woodinville, WA 98072-8478 USA
www.martingale-pub.com

Printed in China
12 11 10 09 08 07   8 7 6 5 4 3 2 1

Library of Congress Cataloging-In-Publication Data
Library of Congress Control Number: 2006035729

ISBN-13: 978-1-56477-717-1

MISSION STATEMENT

Dedicated to providing quality products and service to inspire creativity.

CONTENTS

INTRODUCTION

MORE SOCKS! This book expands on my first sock book, **Sensational Knitted Socks**. There are indeed more sock patterns, more entries in the stitch dictionary, more ways to construct your socks—top down or toe up for most of them—and a choice of heel and toe styles for all the socks. This book allows you to design your own socks—selecting yarn, gauge, decorative pattern, heel, toe, cuff, special-fit options, and reinforcing where needed.

Like the first book, **More Sensational Knitted Socks** encourages you to participate and create socks your way. You choose the yarn you like, knit at a gauge that satisfies you, pick the pattern and the size, and decide whether to reinforce or not. All the calculations were done based on the width of the decorative pattern. All you have to do is knit!

This book does not contain a Class Sock, per se—the basic sock I teach in my beginning sock classes. If you want to knit a sample sock, try a new direction, heel, or toe before you embark on your precious sock yarn, try knitting the smallest size of the chosen sock. You can shorten the leg and foot to get the practice you need before knitting the real sock.

Included in this book is a four-stitch sock pattern written for narrow and wide heels as well as a standard heel. Instructions are also given for adding reinforcing thread and working additional heel stitches to reinforce areas that may wear out faster.

Finally, there are some fun, colorful socks for you to try so you can play with the patterns and lots of colors. I hope you have as much fun with them as I did.

SPECIALTY SOCKS

There are some knitters who think that they need a "special" pattern for special socks. You can use a standard pattern and make a few changes to make them the specialty type that you want. Here are a few with suggestions on how to knit them.

Bed socks. These are a wonderful idea on a cool night. Since wearing socks to bed does not produce wear points, you can knit with soft yarns that might not last long if you did a lot of walking, so here is your chance to knit with 100% alpaca (see the four-stitch repeat pink sock on page 10), silk, cashmere, or merino. They feel truly luxurious and will keep those toes warm all winter long.

Men's socks. Generally, men's socks are knit larger than women's socks, in darker and more subdued colors, with simpler and probably not lacy patterns. There are many options for knitting for men in these patterns; two of the socks were knit by John Jarvis, one using Tuffy, which would make a wonderful hiking sock, and one using fingering-weight yarn in a simple rib suitable to wear with a suit. For special fit or durability hints, see "Four-Stitch Patterns for Narrow and Wide Heels" on page 16. John Jarvis suggested to me that if the wearer has a relatively narrow ankle and generous calf, knit the cuff with a stretchy ribbing for longer than the 1½" suggested so the socks stay up better.

Stansfield 12 sock made with Essential from Knit Picks (color 23696 Ash) on size 1 needles with a gauge of 8½ sts to 1". See "Four-Stitch Patterns."

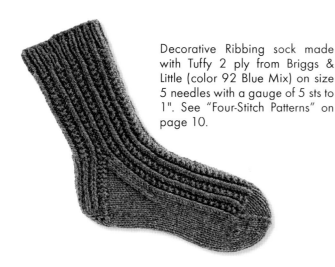

Decorative Ribbing sock made with Tuffy 2 ply from Briggs & Little (color 92 Blue Mix) on size 5 needles with a gauge of 5 sts to 1". See "Four-Stitch Patterns" on page 10.

Children's socks. This is a matter of size and style. For kid's socks, it is fun to make multicolored socks with perhaps different cuffs, heels, and toes (a good use for those leftovers from your own socks). But bright, fun colors are always right.

Golf or tennis socks. These are available commercially and tend to have a cuff and no leg. So just cast on and use a K2, P2 or K3, P3 rib, for an inch or two, and then work the heel and the foot. The reason for the short cuff and no leg—no tan lines on the lower leg.

Dance or yoga socks. These socks do not have heels or toes. The wearer has more traction on a bare wood floor. Knit the cuff you like, then when you get to the point where you would work a heel, bind off the heel stitches loosely (see page 77 for stretchy bind-off options). Cast on the same number of stitches immediately (this is a short-row heeled sock minus the heel), and work the foot until about 1½" before you would begin the toe. Work the last 1½" in a stretchy rib such as K2, P2, and bind off loosely. The rib at the end will keep the socks from sliding toward the heel and curling.

Be expansive in your view of covering your feet. Just because there isn't a written pattern doesn't mean you can't knit it.

HOW TO USE THIS BOOK

1. Read all the information on pages 6–9.

2. Select the sock and then the stitch pattern you want to make. Because you can decide to make most socks top down or toe up, look at the little stitch pictures carefully to determine if you like the way the pattern looks as it will appear on the sock.

3. Measure your foot or the recipient's foot. Or use the size charts on pages 82–83 to determine foot circumference.

4. In the project directions, refer to the stitch table for a range of appropriate gauges. Make sure the yarn you've selected will give you a satisfactory sock.

5. Knit a gauge swatch.

6. Determine how many stitches to cast on by checking the stitch table as follows. Find your gauge in the far-left column; then follow that row until you reach your foot circumference. If there's a number in the intersecting cell, that number indicates how many stitches you should cast on. If the cell is blank, refer to the "Sock Stitches" table on page 7.

7. Familiarize yourself with the pattern. Highlight the stitch counts for the size you are making. For example, there are 12 sizes in the Four-Stitch Patterns sock on page 11. If yours is the sock with a cast on of 64 stitches, which is the fifth number in the set of 12, you'll follow the stitch counts in the fifth position throughout the directions. You might want to photocopy the pattern for marking up.

8. Decide if you're going to work from the top down or toe up and which style heel you want to knit. Read the pattern so you're familiar with all the parts you need to knit. Also decide if you're going to substitute any elements, such as cast ons, bind offs, heel stitch, and so on, and make a note of it in your pattern.

9. Cast on and follow the directions in the appropriate column.

READING STITCH COUNTS IN PATTERN CHARTS

As you look through the directions for the various sock patterns, you'll see the phrase "sts per needles" followed by a series of numbers in parentheses. The numbers within each set of parentheses apply to a specific sock size.

For example, in the four-dpn method, (8, 8, 16) are the numbers on needles 1, 2, and 3 for the 32-stitch cast on, and (10, 10, 20) are the numbers for the 40-stitch cast on, and so on for each different cast-on number.

In the five-dpn method, if you see simply 8 (10, 12, 14, etc.), it means the stitches are divided evenly over all four needles. For the 32-stitch cast on, that would be 8 stitches each on needles 1, 2, 3, and 4; for the 40-stitch cast on, that would be 10 stitches each on needles 1, 2, 3, and 4; and so on.

And likewise, in the two-circular-needles method, 16 (20, 24, 28, etc.) means that the stitches are divided evenly over the two needles. For the 32-stitch cast on, that would be 16 stitches each on needles 1 and 2.

So remember, when you see several sets of parentheses, the numbers within each set of parentheses relate to a specific sock size. When you see a single number, followed by a set of numbers in parentheses, it means that each number relates to a specific sock size, and those stitches are divided evenly over the number of needles in that technique.

SOCK STITCH TABLES

With a little help from lots of tables, you will have the ability to knit socks in a wide range of sizes and yarns and in a variety of stitch-pattern repeats. Let's look at the chart for a four-stitch pattern repeat.

The top row shows the circumference of the foot in ½" increments. To find the circumference, measure around the widest part of the foot with a tape measure. The column on the far left indicates the stitch gauges over 1", also in ½" increments. The body of the table gives you the number of required sock stitches. Notice that some cells are blank; you'll find out why below.

Let's take a hypothetical sock. The foot circumference is 8" and the gauge is 8 stitches to 1". Reading the chart, we see that we would follow the pattern for 64 stitches. If you do not have a foot that is exactly an even inch or half inch, and neither is your gauge, multiply your foot circumference times your gauge and choose the number that is closest. For example, let's say we have an 8¼" foot and knitted gauge of 7¾". Doing the multiplication, we get a result of 63.93. Round to the nearest whole number and you can see that you use the 64-stitch sock.

What to do if you have a foot with an 8" circumference and a gauge of 7½"? If you look at the chart, the space is blank. If we do the math, we find that the result is 60. Well if 60 is divisible by 4, why is it not on the chart? Because 60 stitches would be 15 repeats of four stitches, which is an odd number of repeats. All the patterns are written so that half of the pattern stitches or repeats are knit on the instep of the sock. You have three options: you can knit the 56-stitch sock (14 repeats), which would be just about ½" smaller, knit the 64-stitch sock (16 repeats), which would be about ½" larger, or you can look in the other pattern sections for a 60-stitch sock. Once you have determined the number of stitches you will use for your sock, check the sizes that are in the instructions. Circle or highlight all your numbers before you begin so that you can keep track of the proper instructions.

Or, if you know that for a particular yarn you always need to cast on a specific number of stitches, then look for a pattern with that stitch count.

NEGATIVE EASE

Some sock knitters like to have their socks fit in a very snug manner. They will measure their foot and take a gauge and then subtract from 5% to 10% or more as negative ease for sock knitting. The socks that they knit typically have a stockinette-stitch foot. I have not included any negative ease in the sock-stitch tables. I find that if I use a ribbed pattern on the leg and instep, any excess fabric is taken up in the elasticity of the pattern and the knitting.

I think that there are a few cautions to think about if using negative ease; when knitting the foot of the sock, make sure it fits; stretching the sock widthwise will make it shorter. If you are knitting only according to the length measurement and have a lot of negative ease, the sock may not be long enough. Additionally, fibers that are under tension—really stretched on the foot—will wear out faster than socks that are relaxed on the foot.

If you want to use negative ease, just multiply the foot circumference times your gauge, subtract the negative ease, and use that number in the patterns.

SOCK STITCHES

Gauge sts/1"	Foot Circumference in Inches														
	5	5½	6	6½	7	7½	8	8½	9	9½	10	10½	11	11½	12
	Number of sts to CO														
5				32			40			48			56		64
5½			32		40	40		48			56			64	64
6		32		40			48		56	56		64	64	72	72
6½	32		40			48		56		64	64		72		
7		40			48		56		64		72	72		80	80
7½				48		56		64		72		80	80	88	88
8	40		48		56		64		72		80		88		96
8½		48		56		64		72		80		88		96	
9		56		64		72		80	88	88	96	96	104	104
9½	48			64		72		80	88		96		104	112	112
10		56			72		80	88		96		104	112		120

NEEDLE TECHNIQUES FOR SOCKS

All but one of the patterns (Four-stitch Patterns for Narrow and Wide Heels) include directions for making the socks with three different needle techniques: four double-pointed needles, five double-pointed needles, and two circular needles. The basics for getting started in each of the needle techniques are provided below. Note that the percentages used below are an example of how the stitches would be divided for a "generic" sock. The percentages may vary for some of the other sock patterns, depending on the pattern repeats. Each pattern will tell you how to divide and work stitches for that pattern.

FOUR DOUBLE-POINTED NEEDLES

Cast on 100% of the stitches onto one of the double-pointed needles. Divide the stitches onto three double-pointed needles as follows:

Needle 1: 25% of stitches (begins with the first stitch you cast on)

Needle 2: 25% of stitches

Needle 3: 50% of stitches

Lay the needles on a flat surface and form a triangle so that needle 1 is on the left and needle 3 is on the right. The working end of the yarn should be attached to the last stitch on needle 3. Make sure that the stitches are not twisted.

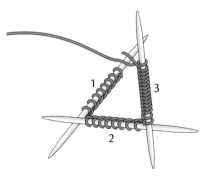

FIVE DOUBLE-POINTED NEEDLES

Cast on 100% of the stitches onto one of the double-pointed needles. Divide the stitches onto four double-pointed needles so that each needle holds 25% of the stitches. Carefully lay the needles on a flat surface and form a rectangle so that needle 1 is on the left and needle 4 is on the right. The working end of the yarn should be attached to the last stitch on needle 4. Make sure that the stitches are not twisted.

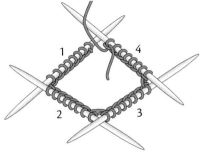

TWO CIRCULAR NEEDLES

Cast on 100% of the stitches onto one of the circular needles. Slip half the stitches to the second needle. Needle 1 holds the first stitches cast on, and needle 2 holds the last stitches cast on and the working end of the yarn.

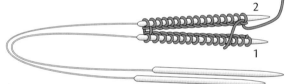

To start knitting on two circular needles, lay both needles on a flat surface with needle 1 closest to you and needle 2 (and the working yarn) away from you. When you knit the stitches on needle 1, you will use both ends of needle 1. Using the working yarn from needle 2, work the first stitch on needle 1 and pull the working yarn snug to close the gap between the two needles. Work the remaining stitches on needle 1. Rotate the work so that you are now ready to work the stitches on needle 2, using both ends of needle 2 to work those stitches. Continue working the cuff pattern around, first on needle 1 and then on needle 2. If you inadvertently use both needles, all the stitches will wind up on one of the needles. It this happens, just slip the stitches back onto the empty needle. Continue working in this manner until the cuff is the desired length. Switch to the leg pattern and continue until the leg is the desired length.

HELPFUL HINTS FOR KNITTING CUSTOM SOCKS

Selecting Yarn. Choose a yarn that is sturdy enough to be walked on and that is simple to launder. Do you love that yarn enough to hand wash those socks?

Casting On and Binding Off Cuffs. There are several good ways that are nonbinding and attractive to cast on (see page 73) and bind off cuffs (see page 77). Try several and don't depend on what you have always done. A new method may be easier or more interesting.

Beginning-of-Round Marker. I use the tail left over from the cast on as a visual reminder that this is the spot for the beginning of the round. You may also use a coilless safety pin to mark this spot.

Picking up Gusset Stitches Along Heel Flap. For a garter-edged heel flap, with right side facing you, pick up the single vertical thread between garter bumps (see page 68). For a chain-selvage-edged heel flap, with right side facing you, pick up one or both loops of the chain selvage (see page 68).

Eliminating the Gusset Gap. To eliminate the gap at the top of the gusset, pick up two extra stitches in the row below where you are working as follows: one stitch from the left half of the stitch that became the heel flap and the other stitch from the right half of the first instep stitch. Both of these stitches will be on the gusset needle (see page 80).

Last Rows of Heel Turn. When working the last two decrease rows of the heel turn, you may end with a decrease; there will be no additional stitch to knit or purl. This is not an error.

Eliminating the Need to Darn Socks. Each person walks in his or her own particular way and hence wears out socks differently.

- Consider using a smaller needle size when knitting heels or toes to make them denser, durable, and longer wearing.

- Attach reinforcing thread (a wool-and-nylon blend that comes with the yarn or is sold separately at yarn stores) when you begin working either the heel flap and turn, or the toes.

- For soles that wear thin, work the foot of the sock on two circulars and use a smaller needle size for the sole than you used for the instep, making a denser and more long-wearing foot.

- For heels that wear out just after the heel turn, consider a toe-up sock with heel flap. The heel flap can be worked on smaller needles or with reinforcing thread to make it more long wearing.

Toe Shaping. The shaping instructions are for "average" feet. If you have pointier or shorter toes than average, then continue working a plain round between decreases for the entire length of the toe; if you have short toes, consider working decrease-only rows sooner.

FOUR-STITCH PATTERNS

The four-stitch patterns are more closely related to K1, P1 than K2, P2. Some of the patterns have the main design consuming three stitches separated by a lone purl. These are the simplest to work, as they are the easiest to memorize and are relaxing to work.

SKILL LEVEL: EASY ■■□□

Seeded Ribbing Check on the leg and plain Seeded Ribbing on the instep made with 100% alpaca wool, fingering weight, from Frog Tree (color 95 Pink) on size 00 needles with a gauge of 8½ sts to 1". The sock is knit from the top down with a garter-edged, eye-of-partridge heel, with the instep pattern continuing onto the standard toe.

Basket Weave sock made with Durasport 1 ply from Briggs and Little (color 91 Blue Jean) on size 2 needles with a gauge of 7 sts to 1". Started at the toe with the Loop de Loop cast on and a round toe, this sock is worked with a short-row heel.

Crossed Ribbing sock made with 100% wool, fingering weight, from Strickwear.com (color Coral Reef) on size 1 needles with a gauge of 8½ sts to 1". Started at the top with a hemmed cuff and knit with a garter-edged stockinette heel flap, this sock finishes with a standard stockinette toe.

MATERIALS

Gather materials for the socks you'd like to make and select the pattern you'd like to use.

DIRECTIONS

Select the number of sts to CO based on the gauge for your yarn and needles and the circumference of the intended foot.

SOCK STITCHES

Gauge sts/1"	Foot Circumference in Inches														
	5	5½	6	6½	7	7½	8	8½	9	9½	10	10½	11	11½	12
	Number of sts to CO														
5				32			40			48			56		64
5½			32		40	40		48			56			64	64
6		32		40			48		56	56		64	64	72	72
6½	32		40			48		56		64	64		72		
7		40			48		56		64		72	72		80	80
7½				48		56		64		72		80	80	88	88
8	40		48		56		64		72		80		88		96
8½		48		56		64		72		80		88		96	
9			56		64		72		80	88	88	96	96	104	104
9½	48			64		72		80	88		96		104	112	112
10		56			72		80	88		96		104	112		120

TOP-DOWN SOCKS

CUFF AND LEG (FOR TOE-UP VERSION, SEE PAGE 14)

Using one of the COs beg on page 73, CO 32 (40, 48, 56, 64, 72, 80, 88, 96, 104, 112, 120) sts. Divide sts per needle as follows:

4 dpn	5 dpn	2 circular needles
(8, 8, 16), (12, 8, 20), (12, 12, 24), (16, 12, 28), (16, 16, 32), (20, 16, 36), (20, 20, 40), (24, 20, 44), (24, 24, 48), (28, 24, 52), (28, 28, 56), (32, 28, 60)	(8, 8, 8, 8), (12, 8, 12, 8), (12, 12, 12, 12), (16, 12, 16, 12), (16, 16, 16, 16), (20, 16, 20, 16), (20, 20, 20, 20), (24, 20, 24, 20), (24, 24, 24, 24), (28, 24, 28, 24), (28, 28, 28, 28), (32, 28, 32, 28)	16 (20, 24, 28, 32, 36, 40, 44, 48, 52, 56, 60)

Join, being careful not to twist sts. Work ribbing for 1½" using suggested ribbing for desired leg pattern (pages 86–87). Work leg to desired length.

HEEL

Work heel on 15 (19, 23, 27, 31, 35, 39, 43, 47, 51, 55, 59) sts, beg with WS row and ending with RS row. Move 1 st from heel to instep as follows to balance patt on instep:

4 dpn	5 dpn	2 circular needles
Unwork last st on needle 3 and place it on needle 1. Needles 1 and 2: Instep sts Needle 3: Heel sts Sts per needle: (9, 8, 15), (13, 8, 19), (13, 12, 23), (17, 12, 27), (17, 16, 31), (21, 16, 35), (21, 20, 39), (25, 20, 43), (25, 24, 47), (29, 24, 51), (29, 28, 55), (33, 28, 59)	Unwork last st on needle 4 and place it on needle 1. Sl all sts from needle 4 to needle 3. Needles 1 and 2: Instep sts Needle 3: Heel sts Sts per needle: (9, 8, 15), (13, 8, 19), (13, 12, 23), (17, 12, 27), (17, 16, 31), (21, 16, 35), (21, 20, 39), (25, 20, 43), (25, 24, 47), (29, 24, 51), (29, 28, 55), (33, 28, 59)	Unwork last st on needle 2 and place it on needle 1. Needle 1: Instep sts Needle 2: Heel sts Sts per needle: (17, 15), (21, 19), (25, 23), (29, 27), (33, 31), (37, 35), (41, 39), (45, 43), (49, 47), (53, 51), (57, 55), (61, 59)

You have a choice here to work "Heel-Flap Heel" (page 12) or "Short-Row Heel" (page 13).

If you are working heel-flap heel, work as follows until you reach short-row instructions, then skip to "Foot."

HEEL-FLAP HEEL

Work one of heel-st patts below or refer to "Heel Flaps" (page 66) for other options.

Turn work to beg heel on WS row.

Eye-of-partridge heel with 3-st garter edge

Rows 1 and 3 (WS): K3, purl to end.

Row 2: P3, *K1, sl 1, rep from * to last 4 sts, K4.

Row 4: P3, *sl 1, K1, rep from * to last 4 sts, sl 1, K3.

Rep rows 1–4 until you've worked 16 (20, 24, 28, 32, 36, 40, 44, 48, 52, 56, 60) heel-flap rows; last row should be a RS row.

St-st heel with 3-st garter edge

Row 1 (WS): K3, purl to end.

Row 2: P3, knit to end.

Rep rows 1 and 2 until you've worked 16 (20, 24, 28, 32, 36, 40, 44, 48, 52, 56, 60) heel-flap rows; last row should be a RS row.

HEEL TURN

Work as follows:

Row 1 (WS): Sl 1, P7 (9, 11, 13, 15, 17, 19, 21, 23, 25, 27, 29), P2tog, P1, turn.

Row 2: Sl 1, K2, ssk, K1, turn. Note that there will be a small gap between working sts that form heel turn and unworked heel sts.

Row 3: Sl 1, purl to within 1 st of gap, P2tog, P1, turn.

Row 4: Sl 1, knit to within 1 st of gap, ssk, K1, turn.

Rep rows 3 and 4, inc 1 additional knit or purl st after the sl 1 until all side sts are worked, end with completed row 4. There should be 9 (11, 13, 15, 17, 19, 21, 23, 25, 27, 29, 31) sts left on heel flap.

For ease of instructions, beg of rnd is now at center of bottom of foot. The needles are renumbered at this point. Needle 1 is beg of rnd and holds all heel sts.

GUSSET

Combine instep sts onto needle 2.	Needles 2 and 3: Instep sts	Needle 1: Heel sts Needle 2: Instep sts

With RS facing you and needle 1, PU and knit 8 (10, 12, 14, 16, 18, 20, 22, 24, 26, 28, 30) sts from side of heel flap. PU and knit 2 sts at top of gusset (see page 80), then

4 dpn	5 dpn	2 circular needles
Needle 2: Work across instep in patt. Needle 3: PU and knit 2 sts at top of gusset, PU and knit 8 (10, 12, 14, 16, 18, 20, 22, 24, 26, 28, 30) sts from side of heel flap, K4 (5, 6, 7, 8, 9, 10, 11, 12, 13, 14, 15) from needle 1. Sts per needle: (15, 17, 14), (18, 21, 17), (21, 25, 20), (24, 29, 23), (27, 33, 26), (30, 37, 29), (33, 41, 32), (36, 45, 35), (39, 49, 38), (42, 53, 41), (45, 57, 44), (48, 61, 47)	Needles 2 and 3: Work across instep in patt. Needle 4: PU and knit 2 sts at top of gusset, PU and knit 8 (10, 12, 14, 16, 18, 20, 22, 24, 26, 28, 30) sts from side of heel flap, K4 (5, 6, 7, 8, 9, 10, 11, 12, 13, 14, 15) from needle 1. Sts per needle: (15, 9, 8, 14), (18, 13, 8, 17), (21, 13, 12, 20), (24, 17, 12, 23), (27, 17, 16, 26), (21, 21, 16, 29), (33, 21, 20, 32), (36, 25, 20, 35), (39, 25, 24, 38), (42, 29, 24, 41), (45, 29, 28, 44), (48, 33, 28, 47)	PM, work 9 (13, 13, 17, 17, 21, 21, 25, 25, 29, 29, 33) instep sts in patt. Needle 2: Work rem instep sts in patt, PM, PU and knit 2 sts at top of gusset, PU and knit 8 (10, 12, 14, 16, 18, 20, 22, 24, 26, 28, 30) sts from side of heel flap, K4 (5, 6, 7, 8, 9, 10, 11, 12, 13, 14, 15) from needle 1. The needles now hold left half and right half of foot sts rather than sts for instep and bottom of foot. Sts per needle: 23 (28, 33, 38, 43, 48, 53, 58, 63, 68, 73, 78)

CLOSE GUSSET TOP

4 dpn	5 dpn	2 circular needles
Needle 1: Knit to last 2 sts, ssk. Needle 2: Work est patt. Needle 3: K2tog, knit to end.	Needle 1: Knit to last 2 sts, ssk. Needles 2 and 3: Work est patt. Needle 4: K2tog, knit to end.	Needle 1: Knit to 2 sts before marker, ssk, SM, work est patt to end. Needle 2: Work est patt to marker, SM, K2tog, knit to end.

GUSSET DECREASE

Rnd 1	**Rnd 1**	**Rnd 1**
Needle 1: Knit to last 3 sts, K2tog, K1. Needle 2: Work est patt. Needle 3: K1, ssk, knit to end.	Needle 1: Knit to last 3 sts, K2tog, K1. Needles 2 and 3: Work est patt. Needle 4: K1, ssk, knit to end.	Needle 1: Knit to 3 sts before marker, K2tog, K1, SM, work est patt. Needle 2: Work est patt to marker, SM, K1, ssk, knit to end.

Rnd 2: Work in est patt on instep, and in St st on sole.

Rep rnds 1 and 2 until 32 (40, 48, 56, 64, 72, 80, 88, 96, 104, 112, 120) total sts rem.

Proceed to "Foot."

SHORT-ROW HEEL

Note that if you work heel sts on 2 needles, unworked sts are not stretched as much as if you use 1 needle. This also lessens the tendency to create gaps at base of heel.

Work heel back and forth on 15 (19, 23, 27, 31, 35, 39, 43, 47, 51, 55, 59) sts, foll instructions for "Short-Row Heel" on page 68. Rep rows 3 and 4 until 5 (7, 9, 11, 13, 13, 15, 17, 19, 21, 21, 23) sts rem unwrapped. End ready for a RS row.

Reverse short-row shaping.

With heel-st yarn, knit across heel, knitting wrap with last st of heel. Work across instep; when you get back to heel sts, knit first heel st with wrap.

FOOT

4 dpn	5 dpn	2 circular needles
Cont St st on needles 1 and 3, and est patt on needle 2 to desired heel-to-toe length.	Cont St st on needles 1 and 4, and est patt on needles 2 and 3 to desired heel-to-toe length.	Rearrange sts so instep sts are on needle 1 and sole sts are on needle 2. Markers are no longer needed. Cont est patt to desired heel-to-toe length.

TOE SHAPING

Typically toes are knit in St st, but you may cont patt from instep through whole toe; either pay attention and work as it flows, or draw patt on graph paper to keep track of where you are.

Even though all patt reps are a multiple of 4 sts, instep and sole have an odd number of sts with instep having 2 more. Decs beg and end on instep so that when you graft final sts tog, there will be an equal number of sts on instep and sole.

Adjust beg of rnd to side of foot as follows:

4 dpn	5 dpn	2 circular needles
Knit sts on needle 1. Renumber needles. Needle 1: Instep sts Needles 2 and 3: Sole sts Sts per needle: (17, 7, 8), (21, 9, 10), (25, 11, 12), (29, 13, 14), (33, 15, 16), (37, 17, 18), (41, 19, 20), (45, 21, 22), (49, 23, 24), (53, 25, 26), (57, 27, 28), (61, 29, 30)	Knit sts on needle 1. Renumber needles. Needles 1 and 2: Instep sts Needles 3 and 4: Sole sts Sts per needle: (9, 8, 7, 8), (13, 8, 9, 10), (13, 12, 11, 12), (17, 12, 13, 14), (17, 16, 15, 16), (21, 16, 17, 18), (21, 20, 19, 20), (25, 20, 21, 22), (25, 24, 23, 24), (29, 24, 25, 26), (29, 28, 27, 28), (33, 28, 29, 30)	Needle 1: Instep sts Needle 2: Sole sts Sts per needle: (17, 15), (21, 19), (25, 23), (29, 27), (33, 31), (37, 35), (41, 39), (45, 43), (49, 47), (53, 51), (57, 55), (61, 59)

Work toe decs as follows:

Rnd 1 Needle 1: K1, ssk, work instep patt to last 3 sts, K2tog, K1. Needle 2: K1, ssk, knit to end. Needle 3: Knit to last 3 sts, K2tog, K1.	**Rnd 1** Needle 1: K1, ssk, work instep patt to end. Needle 2: Work instep patt to last 3 sts, K2tog, K1. Needle 3: K1, ssk, knit to end. Needle 4: Knit to last 3 sts, K2tog, K1.	**Rnd 1** Needle 1: K1, ssk, work instep patt to last 3 sts, K2tog, K1. Needle 2: K1, ssk, knit to last 3 sts, K2tog, K1.

Rnd 2: Knit around.

Rep rnds 1 and 2 until 16 (20, 24, 28, 32, 36, 40, 44, 48, 52, 56, 60) total sts rem. Sts for instep and sole are as follows: (9, 7), (11, 9), (13, 11), (15, 13), (17, 15), (19, 17), (21, 19), (23, 21), (25, 23), (27, 25), (29, 27), (31, 29).

Rep rnd 1 only until 10 (14, 14, 18, 18, 22, 22, 26, 26, 30, 30, 34) total sts rem. Sts for instep and sole are as follows: 5 (7, 7, 9, 9, 11, 11, 13, 13, 15, 15, 17); last 2 dec will be on instep.

Place instep sts on 1 needle and sole sts on 2nd needle. Graft sts tog with kitchener st (page 79).

TOE-UP INSTRUCTIONS

Use foll instructions for toe-up sock. Then follow instructions specifically for parts of top-down sock as indicated. "Easy Toe" instructions are given here. For a few sizes, the instructions are given for "Round Toe" on page 70.

EASY TOE

With waste yarn and provisional CO (see page 76), CO 6 (8, 10, 12, 12, 14, 16, 18, 20, 20, 22, 24) sts. Purl 1 row with sock yarn.

Work back and forth in St st for 6 rows or until rectangle is approx ½" high, ending on a purl row; call the needle with these sts needle A for 4 dpn and 5 dpn, and needle 1 for 2 circulars. Unzip provisional CO sts, place sts on spare needle. Beg knitting in rnd.

4 dpn	5 dpn	2 circular needles
With RS facing you, K6 (8, 10, 12, 12, 14, 16, 18, 20, 20, 22, 24) from needle A; cont with needle 1, PU and knit 2 sts from side edge. With needle 2, PU and knit 2 sts from side edge, K3 (4, 5, 6, 6, 7, 8, 9, 10, 10, 11, 12) from spare needle. With needle 3, K3 (4, 5, 6, 6, 7, 8, 9, 10, 10, 11, 12) from spare needle, then knit 2 sts from side edge. With last needle, PU and knit 2 sts from side edge, then knit rem sts from needle 1. Complete rnd by knitting across needles 2 and 3. Sts per needle: (10, 5, 5), (12, 6, 6), (14, 7, 7), (16, 8, 8), (16, 8, 8), (18, 9, 9), (20, 10, 10), (22, 11, 11), (24, 12, 12), (24, 12, 12), (26, 13, 13), (28, 14, 14).	With RS facing you, K3 (4, 5, 6, 6, 7, 8, 9, 10, 10, 11, 12) from needle A; these sts will be part of needle 1. With needle 2, K3 (4, 5, 6, 6, 7, 8, 9, 10, 10, 11, 12) from needle A, then PU and knit 2 sts from side edge. With needle 3, PU and knit 2 more sts from side edge, K3 (4, 5, 6, 6, 7, 8, 9, 10, 10, 11, 12) from spare needle. With needle 4, K3 (4, 5, 6, 6, 7, 8, 9, 10, 10, 11, 12) from spare needle, then PU and knit 2 sts from side edge. With needle 5, PU and knit last 2 sts from side edge, K3 (4, 5, 6, 6, 7, 8, 9, 10, 10, 11, 12) from needle 1; these sts will be on needle 1. Complete rnd by knitting across needles 2, 3, and 4. Sts per needle: 5 (6, 7, 8, 8, 9, 10, 11, 12, 12, 13, 14)	With RS facing you, K6 (8, 10, 12, 12, 14, 16, 18, 20, 20, 22, 24); cont with needle 1, PU and knit 2 sts from side edge. With needle 2, PU and knit 2 sts from side edge, K6 (8, 10, 12, 12, 14, 16, 18, 20, 20, 22, 24) from CO edge, PU and knit 2 sts from side edge. With needle 1, PU and knit 2 sts from side edge. Complete rnd by knitting across rem sts on needle 1 and across needle 2. Sts per needle: 10 (12, 14, 16, 16, 18, 20, 22, 24, 24, 26, 28).

Work toe incs as follows:		
Rnd 1 Needle 1: K1, M1, knit to last st, M1, K1. Needle 2: K1, M1, knit to end. Needle 3: Knit to last st, M1, K1.	**Rnd 1** Needle 1: K1, M1, knit to end. Needle 2: Knit to last st, M1, K1. Needle 3: K1, M1, knit to end. Needle 4: Knit to last st, M1, K1.	**Rnd 1** Needle 1: K1, M1, knit to last st, M1, K1. Needle 2: K1, M1, knit to last st, M1, K1.
Rnd 2: Knit around. Rep rnds 1 and 2 until 32 (40, 48, 56, 64, 72, 80, 88, 96, 104, 112, 120) total sts rem. Rearrange sts by moving 1 st from sole to instep. This extra st on instep allows you to balance patt in instep. Work patt of choice on instep until foot is desired length.		
Needle 1: Instep sts Needles 2 and 3: Sole sts Sts per needle: (17, 7, 8), (21, 9, 10), (25, 11, 12), (29, 13, 14), (33, 15, 16), (37, 17, 18), (41, 19, 20), (45, 21, 22), (49, 23, 24), (53, 25, 26), (57, 27, 28), (61, 29, 30)	Needles 1 and 2: Instep sts Needles 3 and 4: Sole sts Sts per needle: (9, 8, 7, 8), (13, 8, 9, 10), (13, 12, 11, 12), (17, 12, 13, 14), (17, 16, 15, 16), (21, 16, 17, 18), (21, 20, 19, 20), (25, 20, 21, 22), (25, 24, 23, 24), (29, 24, 25, 26), (29, 28, 27, 28), (33, 28, 29, 30)	Needle 1: Instep sts Needle 2: Sole sts Sts per needle: (17, 15), (21, 19), (25, 23), (29, 27), (33, 31), (37, 35), (41, 39), (45, 43), (49, 47), (53, 51), (57, 55), (61, 59)
Work patt of choice on instep sts until foot is desired length.		
4 dpn	5 dpn	2 circular needles
Combine sole sts onto needle 3, to become heel sts. Divide instep sts onto needles 1 and 2.	Combine sole sts onto needle 3, to become heel sts.	Sole sts are now heel sts.
HEEL		
Work "Heel-Flap Heel" (page 12) or "Short-Row Heel" (page 13) on heel sts. When you have completed heel and gusset or short-row heel and 32 (40, 48, 56, 64, 72, 80, 88, 96, 104, 112, 120) total sts rem, rearrange sts as follows:		
(8, 8, 16), (10, 10, 20), (12, 12, 24), (14, 14, 28), (16, 16, 32), (18, 18, 36), (20, 20, 40), (22, 22, 44), (24, 24, 48), (26, 26, 52), (28, 28, 56), (30, 30, 60)	8 (10, 12, 14, 16, 18, 20, 22, 24, 26, 28, 30)	16 (20, 24, 28, 32, 36, 40, 44, 48, 52, 56, 60)
LEG		
Discontinue working extra st on instep patt and cont patt around leg to desired length.		
CUFF		
Work cuff for 1½" using suggested ribbing for leg patt you worked. BO loosely (page 77).		

FOUR-STITCH PATTERNS FOR NARROW AND WIDE HEELS

Eyelet Bar with narrow heel sock made with Meilenweit 6 fach from Lana Grossa (color 32 Pink) on size 2 needles with a gauge of 7¾ sts to 1". The heel is garter-edged heel stitch, which continues on the heel turn and on the sole through the gusset for added durability and finishes with a standard toe.

Decorative Ribbing with wide heel sock made with Meilenweit 6 fach from Lana Grossa (color 37 Blue) on size 2 needles with a gauge of 7¾ sts to 1". This heel is garter-edged heel stitch, worked on 60% of the sock stitches to accommodate a wider heel. The heel stitch continues on the heel turn and on the sole through the gusset for added durability.

The instructions for this sock provide numbers as in the four-stitch ribbing patterns. All instructions are written for five double-pointed needles, a compromise between four double-pointed needles and two circular needles. If you check the instructions for four double-pointed needles or two circular needles from the previous pattern, you should be able to make the conversion if you wish.

The heel for the narrow-heeled sock is worked on 40% of the total stitches instead of 50%. The heel for the wide-heeled sock is worked on 60% of the total stitches instead of 50%. The numbers for the heels may not be exactly 40% or 60%, but were adjusted to keep complete pattern repeats on the instep.

Read through the following descriptions of wide and narrow heels to see if you need one of these patterns.

Wide heels. Some people have thick heels, which results in them having difficulty pulling the sock over their heel. Or, if there is not enough fabric to go around the heel, the sock will sag, and eventually a good portion will be down in the shoe instead of around the ankle. The standard sock pattern is written using half of the stitches for the heel. Making the heel flap with 60% of the total sock stitches should alleviate this problem. Even though you have a sock with more stitches in the heel flap, it does not require more rows to be worked. For example, if the sock has 64 stitches, 60% of that is 38.4. I would look at the pattern and see how it centers and probably use 39 stitches for the heel flap. Then knit 32 heel-flap rows, which is standard for a 64-stitch sock. Using 38 stitches for the heel flap will leave 25 stitches for the instep. Work these stitches in the instep pattern. When you get to the toe, knit one round and rearrange the stitches so that there are 32 for the sole and 32 for the instep.

Narrow heels. This is a person who has a narrow heel and a wider ball of the foot. It is best to use a fairly stretchy pattern that will accommodate the width at the toe, yet not bunch up in the foot, where it is narrower. It may also help to work the heel on 40% of the total stitches. Using the 64-stitch example again, use 26 sts for the heel and leave 38 on the instep. Again, you need to work 32 heel-flap rows so that the heel flap is long enough. When you are ready to work the toe, work one round in plain knit and rearrange the stitches for a normal toe.

MATERIALS

Gather materials for the socks you'd like to make and select the pattern you'd like to use.

DIRECTIONS

Select the number of sts to CO based on the gauge for your yarn and needles and the circumference of the intended foot.

SOCK STITCHES

Gauge sts/1"	Foot Circumference in Inches														
	5	5½	6	6½	7	7½	8	8½	9	9½	10	10½	11	11½	12
	Number of sts to CO														
5				32			40			48			56		64
5½			32		40	40		48			56			64	64
6		32		40			48		56	56		64	64	72	72
6½	32		40			48		56		64	64		72		
7		40			48		56		64		72	72		80	80
7½			48			56		64		72		80	80	88	88
8	40		48		56		64		72		80		88		96
8½		48		56		64		72		80		88		96	
9			56		64		72		80	88	88	96	96	104	104
9½	48			64		72		80	88		96		104	112	112
10		56			72		80	88		96		104	112		120

CUFF AND LEG *(All instructions are written for 5 dpn.)*

Using one of the COs beg on page 73, CO 32 (40, 48, 56, 64, 72, 80, 88, 96, 104, 112, 120) sts. Divide sts per needle as follows:

(8, 8, 8, 8), (12, 8, 12, 8), (12, 12, 12, 12), (16, 12, 16, 12), (16, 16, 16, 16), (20, 16, 20, 16), (20, 20, 20, 20), (24, 20, 24, 20), (24, 24, 24, 24), (28, 24, 28, 24), (28, 28, 28, 28), (32, 28, 32, 28)

Join, being careful not to twist sts. Work ribbing for 1½" using suggested ribbing for desired leg pattern (pages 86–87). Work leg to desired length.

HEEL FLAP

If you tend to wear out your socks at the heel, change to a smaller needle or attach reinforcing thread at this point for a more durable heel.

Narrow Heel (5 dpn)	Standard Heel (5 dpn)	Wide Heel (5 dpn)
Work heel on 11 (15, 19, 23, 23, 27, 31, 35, 39, 39, 43, 47) sts, beg with WS row and ending with RS row.	Work heel on 15 (19, 23, 27, 31, 35, 39, 43, 47, 51, 55, 59) sts, beg with WS row and ending with RS row.	Work heel on 19 (23, 27, 31, 39, 43, 47, 51, 55, 63, 67, 71) sts, beg with WS row and ending with RS row.

Rearrange sts to center patt over instep by unworking last st from needle 4 and placing it on needle 1.

Slip all sts from needle 4 to needle 3.

Needles 1 and 2: Instep sts

Needle 3: Heel sts

Sts per needle: (9, 8, 15), (11, 10, 19), (13, 12, 23), (15, 14, 27), (17, 16, 31), (19, 18, 35), (21, 20, 39), (23, 22, 43), (25, 24, 47), (27, 26, 51), (29, 28, 55), (31, 30, 59)

	Sts per needle: (9, 8, 15), (11, 10, 19), (13, 12, 23), (15, 14, 27), (17, 16, 31), (19, 18, 35), (21, 20, 39), (23, 22, 43), (25, 24, 47), (27, 26, 51), (29, 28, 55), (31, 30, 59)	
Rearrange sts to create fewer sts for a narrower heel. Move 4 (4, 4, 4, 8, 8, 8, 8, 8, 12, 12, 12) sts from needle 3 to needle 2. Sts per needle: (9, 12, 11), (13, 12, 15), (13, 16, 19), (17, 16, 23), (17, 24, 23), (21, 24, 27), (21, 28, 31), (25, 28, 35), (25, 32, 39), (29, 36, 39), (29, 40, 43), (33, 40, 47) Some sizes have unbalanced patt reps; on instep, move 0 (0, 0, 0, 4, 0, 4, 0, 4, 4, 8, 4) sts from needle 2 to needle 1. Sts per needle: (9, 12, 11), (13, 12, 15), (13, 16, 19), (17, 16, 23), (21, 20, 23), (21, 24, 27), (25, 24, 31), (25, 28, 35), (29, 28, 39), (33, 32, 39), (37, 32, 43), (37, 36, 47)		Rearrange sts to move more sts for a wider heel. Move 4 (4, 4, 4, 8, 8, 8, 8, 12, 12, 12) sts from needle 2 to needle 3. Sts per needle: (9, 4, 19), (13, 4, 23), (13, 8, 27), (17, 8, 31), (17, 8, 39), (21, 8, 43), (21, 12, 47), (25, 12, 51), (25, 16, 55), (29, 12, 63), (29, 16, 67), (33, 16, 71) Some sizes have unbalanced patt reps; on instep move 0 (4, 0, 4, 4, 4, 4, 4, 8, 4, 8) sts from needle 1 to needle 2. Sts per needle: (9, 4, 19), (9, 8, 23), (13, 8, 27), (13, 12, 31), (13, 12, 39), (17, 12, 43), (17, 16, 47), (21, 16, 51), (21, 20, 55), (21, 20, 63), (25, 20, 67), (25, 24, 71)

Turn work to beg heel on WS row.

Heel stitch with 3-st garter edge

Row 1 (WS): K3, purl to end.

Row 2: P3, *K1, sl 1, rep from * to last 4 sts, K4.

Rep rows 1 and 2 until you have 16 (20, 24, 28, 32, 36, 40, 44, 48, 52, 56, 60) heel-flap rows; last row should be RS row.

HEEL TURN

Row 1 (WS): Sl 1, P6 (8, 10, 12, 12, 14, 16, 18, 20, 20, 22, 24), P2tog, P1, turn.	**Row 1 (WS):** Sl 1, P8 (10, 12, 14, 16, 18, 20, 22, 24, 26, 28, 30), P2tog, P1, turn.	**Row 1 (WS):** Sl 1, P10 (12, 14, 16, 20, 22, 24, 26, 28, 32, 34, 36), P2tog, P1, turn.

To make heel turn and center of bottom of foot more durable, you may cont heel st on heel turn and on center of bottom of foot. If you want to work heel turn with St st, just knit sts between first slipped stitch and ssk on even-numbered rows of heel turn.

Row 2: Sl 1, K1, sl 1, K1, sl 1, ssk, K1, turn. Note that there will be a small gap between working sts that form heel turn and unworked heel sts.

Row 3: Sl 1, purl to within 1 st of gap, P2tog, P1, turn.

Row 4: Sl 1, K2, *sl 1, K1, rep from * to within 1 st of gap, ssk, K1, turn.

Row 5: Sl 1, purl to within 1 st of gap, P2tog, P1, turn.

Row 6: Sl 1, K1, *sl 1, K1, rep from * to within 1 st of gap, ssk, K1, turn.

Rep rows 3, 4, 5, and 6, inc 1 additional knit or purl st after the sl 1 until all side sts are worked; end with completed row 4. Note that there may not be a K1 or P1 in last 2 rows of heel turn.

| There should be 7 (9, 11, 13, 13, 15, 17, 19, 21, 21, 23, 25) sts left on heel flap. | There should be 9 (11, 13, 15, 17, 19, 21, 23, 25, 27, 29, 31) sts left on heel flap. | There should be 11 (13, 15, 17, 21, 23, 25, 27, 29, 33, 35, 37) sts left on heel flap. |

For ease of instructions, beg of rnd is now at center of bottom of foot. The needles are renumbered at this point. Needle 1 is beg of rnd and holds all heel sts.

GUSSET

If you switched to a smaller needle for heel flap, change back to original size now.

Narrow Heel (5 dpn)	Standard Heel (5 dpn)	Wide Heel (5 dpn)

PM before you pick up sts. With RS facing you and needle 1, PU and knit 8 (10, 12, 14, 16, 18, 20, 22, 24, 26, 28, 30) sts from side of heel flap, PU and knit 2 sts at top of gusset (see page 80).

| Needles 2 and 3: Work across instep in patt.

Needle 4: PU and knit 2 sts at top of gusset, PU and knit 8 (10, 12, 14, 16, 18, 20, 22, 24, 26, 28, 30) sts from side of heel flap, PM, K3 (4, 5, 6, 6, 7, 8, 9, 10, 10, 11, 12) heel sts.

Sts per needle (you may need to rearrange sts): (14, 9, 12, 13), (17, 13, 12, 16), (20, 17, 12, 19), (23, 17, 16, 22), (25, 17, 24, 24), (28, 21, 24, 27), (31, 21, 28, 30), (34, 29, 24, 33), (37, 25, 32, 36), (39, 33, 32, 38), (42, 29, 40, 41), (45, 33, 40, 44) | Needles 2 and 3: Work across instep in patt.

Needle 4: PU and knit 2 sts at top of gusset, PU and knit 8 (10, 12, 14, 16, 18, 20, 22, 24, 26, 28, 30) sts from side of heel flap, PM, K4 (5, 6, 7, 8, 9, 10, 11, 12, 13, 14, 15) heel sts.

Sts per needle (you may need to rearrange sts): (15, 9, 8, 14), (18, 9, 12, 17), (21, 13, 12, 20), (24, 13, 16, 23), (27, 17, 16, 26), (30, 17, 20, 29), (33, 21, 20, 32), (36, 21, 24, 35), (39, 25, 24, 38), (42, 25, 28, 41), (45, 29, 28, 44), (48, 29, 32, 47) | Needles 2 and 3: Work across instep in patt.

Needle 4: PU and knit 2 sts at top of gusset, then PU and knit 8 (10, 12, 14, 16, 18, 20, 22, 24, 26, 28, 30) sts from side of heel flap, PM, K5 (6, 7, 8, 10, 11, 12, 13, 14, 16, 17, 18) heel sts.

Sts per needle (you may need to rearrange sts): (16, 9, 4, 15), (19, 9, 8, 18), (22, 13, 8, 21), (25, 13, 12, 24), (29, 17, 8, 28), (32, 17, 12, 31), (35, 21, 12, 34), (38, 21, 16, 37), (41, 25, 16, 40), (45, 25, 16, 44), (48, 29, 16, 47), (51, 29, 20, 50) |

CLOSE GUSSET TOP

Needle 1: Knit to last 2 sts, ssk.

Needles 2 and 3: Work est patt.

Needle 4: K2tog, knit to end of needle.

GUSSET DECREASES

Rnd 1

Needle 1: Work est heel st to marker, SM, knit to last 3 sts, K2tog, K1.

Needles 2 and 3: Work est patt.

Needle 4: K1, ssk, knit to marker, work est heel st to end.

Rnd 2

Needle 1: Knit.

Needles 2 and 3: Work est patt.

Needle 4: Knit.

Rep rnds 1 and 2 until 32 (40, 48, 56, 64, 72, 80, 88, 96, 104, 112, 120) total sts rem.

Sts per needle:

| (6, 9, 12, 5), (8, 13, 12, 7), (10, 17, 12, 9), (12, 17, 16, 11), (12, 17, 24, 11), (14, 21, 24, 13), (16, 21, 28, 15), (18, 29, 24, 17), (20, 25, 32, 19), (20, 33, 32, 19), (22, 29, 40, 21), (24, 33, 40, 23) | (8, 9, 8, 7), (10, 9, 12, 9), (12, 13, 12, 11), (14, 13, 16, 13), (16, 17, 16, 15), (18, 17, 20, 17), (20, 21, 20, 19), (22, 21, 24, 21), (24, 25, 24, 23), (26, 25, 28, 25), (28, 29, 28, 27), (30, 29, 32, 29) | (10, 9, 4, 9), (12, 9, 8, 11), (14, 13, 8, 13), (16, 13, 12, 15), (20, 17, 8, 19), (22, 17, 12, 21), (24, 21, 12, 23), (26, 21, 16, 25), (28, 25, 16, 27), (32, 25, 16, 31), (34, 29, 16, 33), (36, 29, 20, 35) |

FOOT
Cont St st on needles 1 and 4 (sole), and est patt on needles 2 and 3 (instep) to desired heel-to-toe length.

TOE SHAPING
Typically toes are knit in St st, but you can cont patt from instep through whole toe; either pay attention and work as it flows, or draw patt on graph paper to keep track of where you are.
To balance patt on instep, which has an odd number of sts, let instep sts have half plus 1 stitch, and sole or bottom of foot have half minus 1 st. The instep has 2 more sts than bottom. Decs beg and end on instep so that when you are ready to graft top and bottom, you will have same number of sts.
Adjust beg of rnd to side of foot as follows:

Narrow Heel (5 dpn)	Standard Heel (5 dpn)	Wide Heel (5 dpn)
Knit sts on needle 1, then work 2 (2, 2, 2, 4, 4, 4, 4, 4, 6, 6, 6) from needle 2 and transfer to needle 1. Work rem sts on needle 2. Work sts on needle 3 and transfer last 2 (2, 2, 2, 4, 4, 4, 4, 4, 6, 6, 6) sts from needle 3 to needle 4.	Knit sts on needle 1. Renumber needles. Needles 1 and 2: Instep sts Needles 3 and 4: Sole sts	Knit sts on needle 1, but when you get to last 2 (2, 2, 2, 4, 4, 4, 4, 4, 6, 6, 6) sts, transfer them to needle 2. Work rem sts on needle 2. Work needle 3 and then work first 2 (2, 2, 2, 4, 4, 4, 4, 4, 6, 6, 6) sts from needle 4 onto needle 3. Work rem sts on needle 4.

STANDARD TOE
For a more durable toe, change to a smaller needle and/or use reinforcing thread for toe.
Arrange sts as follows:
Needles 1 and 2: Instep sts
Needles 3 and 4: Sole sts
Sts per needle: (8, 9, 7, 8), (10, 11, 9, 10), (12, 13, 11, 12), (14, 15, 13, 14), (16, 17, 15, 16), (18, 19, 17, 18), (20, 21, 19, 20), (22, 23, 21, 22), (24, 25, 23, 24), (26, 27, 25, 26), (28, 29, 27, 28), (30, 31, 29, 30)
Work toe decs as follows:

Rnd 1

Needle 1: K1, ssk, work instep patt to end.

Needle 2: Work instep patt to last 3 sts, K2tog, K1.

Needle 3: K1, ssk, knit to end.

Needle 4: Knit to last 3 sts, K2tog, K1.

Rnd 2: Knit around.

Rep rnds 1 and 2 until 16 (20, 24, 28, 32, 36, 40, 44, 48, 52, 56, 60) total sts rem. Sts for instep and sole are as follows: (9, 7), (11, 9), (13, 11), (15, 13), (17, 15), (19, 17), (21, 19), (23, 21), (25, 23), (27, 25), (29, 27), (31, 29).

Rep rnd 1 only until 10 (14, 14, 18, 18, 22, 22, 26, 26, 30, 30, 34) total sts rem. Sts for instep and sole are as follows: 5 (7, 7, 9, 9, 11, 11, 13, 13, 15, 15, 17); last 2 dec will be on instep.

Place instep sts on 1 needle and sole sts on 2nd needle. Graft sts tog with kitchener st (page 79).

FIVE-STITCH PATTERNS

The basic pattern structure for these socks is a pattern of interest of four stitches with an extra stitch separating the interest. It is fun to make up your own ribbing for these patterns because standard ribbings won't line up with the pattern.

SKILL LEVEL: EASY ◖■□□

Sailor's Ribbing sock made with Jawoll Superwash from Lang Yarns (color 78 Dutch Blue) on size 1 needles with a gauge of 9 sts to 1". The sock starts at the top with ribbing that blends with the leg pattern and continues to a garter-edged heel that continues the leg pattern and ends with a stockinette standard toe.

Ridged Squares sock made with Tuffy 2 ply from Briggs & Little (color 95 Red Mix) on size 5 needles with a gauge of 5¼ sts to 1". Started at the top, these socks are made with a garter-edged, stockinette-stitch heel and finished with a standard toe.

Vertical Eyelets sock made with Gems Merino Opal from Louet Sales (color 54 Teal) on size 2 needles with a gauge of 7 sts to 1". Started at the toe with the "Easy Toe," these socks are worked with a short-row heel and finished with the picot bind off.

MATERIALS

Gather materials for the socks you'd like to make and select the pattern you'd like to use.

DIRECTIONS

Select the number of sts to CO based on the gauge for your yarn and needles and the circumference of the intended foot.

SOCK STITCHES

Foot Circumference in Inches — Number of sts to CO

Gauge sts/1"	5	5½	6	6½	7	7½	8	8½	9	9½	10	10½	11	11½	12
5			30				40				50				60
5½		30				40			50				60		
6	30			40				50			60			70	
6½			40			50			60				70		80
7		40			50			60			70			80	
7½		40		50			60			70		80			90
8	40		50	50		60		70	70		80		90	90	
8½			50		60		70			80		90			100
9		50		60			70		80		90		100		110
9½		50		60		70		80		90		100		110	
10	50		60		70		80		90		100		110		120

All 5-st patts have even number of sts so full-patt reps are on instep with equal number of sts on sole.

TOP-DOWN SOCKS

CUFF AND LEG (FOR TOE-UP VERSION, SEE PAGE 25)

Using one of the COs beg on page 73, CO 30 (40, 50, 60, 70, 80, 90, 100, 110, 120) sts. Divide sts per needle as follows:

4 dpn	5 dpn	2 circular needles
(10, 5, 15), (10, 10, 20), (15, 10, 25), (15, 15, 30), (20, 15, 35), (20, 20, 40), (25, 20, 45), (25, 25, 50), (30, 25, 55), (30, 30, 60)	(10, 5, 10, 5), (10, 10, 10, 10), (15, 10, 15, 10), (15, 15, 15, 15), (20, 15, 20, 15), (20, 20, 20, 20), (25, 20, 25, 20), (25, 25, 25, 25), (30, 25, 30, 25), (30, 30, 30, 30)	15 (20, 25, 30, 35, 40, 45, 50, 55, 60)

Join, being careful not to twist sts. Work ribbing for 1½" using suggested ribbing for desired leg pattern (pages 88–90). Work leg to desired length.

HEEL

Work heel on 14 (19, 24, 29, 34, 39, 44, 49, 54, 59) sts, beg with WS row and ending with RS row. Move 1 st from heel to instep as follows to balance patt on instep:

Unwork last st on needle 3 and place it on needle 1. Needles 1 and 2: Instep sts Needle 3: Heel sts Sts per needle: (11, 5, 14), (11, 10, 19), (16, 10, 24), (16, 15, 29), (21, 15, 34), (21, 20, 39), (26, 20, 44), (26, 25, 49), (31, 25, 54), (31, 30, 59)	Unwork last st on needle 4 and place it on needle 1. Sl all sts from needle 4 to needle 3. Needles 1 and 2: Instep sts Needle 3: Heel sts. Sts per needle: (11, 5, 14), (11, 10, 19), (16, 10, 24), (16, 15, 29), (21, 15, 34), (21, 20, 39), (26, 20, 44), (26, 25, 49), (31, 25, 54), (31, 30, 59)	Unwork last st on needle 2 and place it on needle 1. Needle 1: Instep sts Needle 2: Heel sts Sts per needle: (16, 14), (21, 19), (26, 24), (31, 29), (36, 34), (41, 39), (46, 44), (51, 49), (56, 54), (61, 59)

You have a choice here to work "Heel-Flap Heel" below or "Short-Row Heel" (page 24). If you are working heel-flap heel, cont working until you reach "Short-Row Heel," then skip to "Foot."

HEEL-FLAP HEEL

Work heel-st patt below or refer to "Heel Flaps" (page 66) for other options.

Turn work to beg heel on WS row.

Note that you will not sl sts at end of rows; this heel does not have a chain selvage.

St-st heel with 3-st garter edge

Row 1 (WS): K3, purl to end.

Row 2: P3, knit to end.

Rep rows 1 and 2 until you have 14 (20, 24, 30, 34, 40, 44, 50, 54, 60) heel-flap rows; last row should be a RS row.

HEEL TURN

Work as follows:

Row 1 (WS): Sl 1, P8 (10, 13, 15, 18, 20, 23, 25, 28, 30), P2tog, P1, turn.

Row 2: Sl 1, K3 (4, 3, 4, 3, 4, 3, 4, 3, 4), ssk, K1, turn. Note that there will be a small gap between working sts that form heel turn and unworked heel sts.

Row 3: Sl 1, purl to within 1 st of gap, P2tog, P1, turn.

Row 4: Sl 1, knit to within 1 st of gap, ssk, K1, turn.

Rep rows 3 and 4, inc 1 additional knit or purl st after the sl 1 until all side sts are worked; end with completed row 4. There should be 9 (11, 15, 16, 19, 22, 25, 28, 29, 32) sts left on heel flap. When working rows 3 and 4, there may be no ending single st to work; some numbers don't work out.

For ease of instructions, beg of rnd is now at center of bottom of foot. The needles are renumbered at this point. Needle 1 is beg of rnd and holds all heel sts.

GUSSET

4 dpn	5 dpn	2 circular needles
Combine instep sts onto needle 2.	Needles 2 and 3: Instep sts	Needle 1: Heel sts Needle 2: Instep sts

With RS facing you and needle 1, PU and knit 7 (10, 12, 15, 17, 20, 22, 25, 27, 30) sts from side of heel flap. PU and knit 2 extra sts at top of gusset (see page 80), then

4 dpn	5 dpn	2 circular needles
Needle 2: Work across instep in patt, beg where you left off in patt to work heel. Needle 3: PU and knit 2 extra sts at top of gusset, PU and knit 7 (10, 12, 15, 17, 20, 22, 25, 27, 30) sts from side of heel flap, K4 (5, 7, 8, 9, 11, 12, 14, 14, 15) from needle 1. Sts per needle: (14, 16, 13), (18, 21, 17), (22, 26, 21), (25, 31, 25), (29, 36, 28), (33, 41, 33), (37, 46, 36), (41, 51, 41), (44, 56, 43), (49, 61, 47)	Needles 2 and 3: Work across instep in patt, beg where you left off in patt to work heel. Needle 4: PU and knit 2 extra sts at top of gusset, PU and knit 7 (10, 12, 15, 17, 20, 22, 25, 27, 30) sts from side of heel flap, K4 (5, 7, 8, 9, 11, 12, 14, 14, 15) from needle 1. Sts per needle: (14, 11, 5, 13), (18, 11, 10, 17), (22, 16, 10, 21), (25, 16, 15, 25), (29, 21, 15, 28), (33, 21, 20, 33), (37, 26, 20, 36), (41, 26, 25, 41), (44, 31, 25, 43), (49, 31, 30, 47)	Cont with needle 1: PM, work 11, (11, 16, 16, 21, 21, 26, 26, 31, 31) sts in patt. Needle 2: Work rem instep sts, PM, PU and knit 2 extra sts at top of gusset, PU and knit 7 (10, 12, 15, 17, 20, 22, 25, 27, 30) sts from side of heel flap, K4 (5, 7, 8, 9, 11, 12, 14, 14, 15) from needle 1. Sts per needle: (25, 18), (29, 27), (38, 31), (41, 40), (50, 43), (54, 52), (63, 56), (67, 66), (75, 68), (80, 77)

CLOSE GUSSET TOP

Needle 1: Knit to last 2 sts, ssk. Needle 2: Work est patt. Needle 3: K2tog, knit to end.	Needle 1: Knit to last 2 sts, ssk. Needles 2 and 3: Work est patt. Needle 4: K2tog, knit to end.	Needle 1: Knit to 2 sts before marker, ssk, SM, work est patt. Needle 2: Work est patt to marker, SM, K2tog, knit to end.

GUSSET DECREASE

4 dpn	5 dpn	2 circular needles
Rnd 1 Needle 1: Knit to last 3 sts, K2tog, K1. Needle 2: Work est patt. Needle 3: K1, ssk, knit to end.	**Rnd 1** Needle 1: Knit to last 3 sts, K2tog, K1. Needles 2 and 3: Work est patt. Needle 4: K1, ssk, knit to end.	**Rnd 1** Needle 1: Knit to 3 sts before marker, K2tog, K1, SM, work est patt. Needle 2: Work est patt to marker, SM, K1, ssk, knit to end.

Rnd 2: Work in est patt on instep, and in St st on sole.

Rep rnds 1 and 2 until 30 (40, 50, 60, 70, 80, 90, 100, 110, 120) total sts rem.

Proceed to "Foot."

SHORT-ROW HEEL

Note that if you work heel sts on 2 needles, unworked sts are not stretched as much as if you use 1 needle. This also lessens the tendency to create gaps at base of heel.

Work heel back and forth on 14 (19, 24, 29, 34, 39, 44, 49, 54, 59) sts, foll instructions for "Short-Row Heel" on page 68.

Rep rows 3 and 4 until 6 (7, 9, 10, 12, 13, 16, 17, 19, 20) sts rem unwrapped, ending with a WS row.

Reverse short-row shaping.

With heel-st yarn, knit across heel, knitting wrap with last st of heel. Work across instep; when you get back to heel sts, knit first heel st with wrap.

FOOT

Cont instep in est patt, and sole in St st to desired heel-to-toe length. Make sure that sts are arranged as follows:

Sts per needle: (16, 5, 9), (21, 10, 9), (26, 10, 14), (31, 15, 14), (36, 15, 19), (41, 20, 19), (46, 20, 24), (51, 25, 24), (56, 25, 29), (61, 30, 29)	Sts per needle: (6, 10, 5, 9), (11, 10, 10, 9), (11, 15, 10, 14), (16, 15, 15, 14), (16, 20, 15, 19), (21, 20, 20, 19), (21, 25, 20, 24), (26, 25, 25, 24), (26, 30, 25, 29), (31, 30, 30, 29)	Sts per needle: (16, 14), (21, 19), (26, 24), (31, 29), (36, 34), (41, 39), (46, 44), (51, 49), (56, 54), (61, 59)

TOE SHAPING

Knit sts on needle 1. Needle 1: Instep sts Needles 2 and 3: Sole sts	Knit sts on needle 1. Needles 1 and 2: Instep sts Needles 3 and 4: Sole sts	Knit to marker. Markers are no longer needed. Needle 1: Instep sts Needle 2: Sole sts

Work dec as follows:

Rnd 1 Needle 1: K1, ssk, work instep patt to last 3 sts, K2tog, K1. Needle 2: K1, ssk, knit to end. Needle 3: Knit to last 3 sts, K2tog, K1.	**Rnd 1** Needle 1: K1, ssk, work instep patt to end. Needle 2: Work instep patt to last 3 sts, K2tog, K1. Needle 3: K1, ssk, knit to end. Needle 4: Knit to last 3 sts, K2tog, K1.	**Rnd 1** Needle 1: K1, ssk, work instep patt to last 3 sts, K2tog, K1. Needle 2: K1, ssk, knit to last 3 sts, K2tog, K1.

Rnd 2: Knit around.

Rep rnds 1 and 2 until 16 (20, 24, 28, 36, 40, 44, 52, 56, 60) total sts rem. Sts for instep and sole are as follows (9, 7), (11, 9), (13, 11), (15, 13), (19, 17), (21, 19), (23, 21), (27, 25), (29, 27), (31, 29).

Rep rnd 1 only until 10 (10, 14, 14, 18, 18, 22, 26, 26, 30) total sts rem. Sts for instep and sole are as follows: 5 (5, 7, 7, 9, 9, 11, 13, 13, 15); last 2 dec will be on instep.

Place instep sts on 1 needle and sole sts on 2nd needle. Graft sts tog with kitchener st (page 79).

TOE-UP SOCKS

If you would like to work this sock from the toe up, follow these instructions for toe, and then follow instructions specifically for parts of top-down socks as indicated.

EASY TOE

With waste yarn and provisional CO (see page 76), CO 6 (8, 10, 12, 14, 16, 18, 20, 22, 24) sts. Purl 1 row with sock yarn.

Work back and forth in St st for 6 rows or until rectangle is approx ½" high; end on a purl row, call the needle with these sts needle A for 4 dpn and 5 dpn, and needle 1 for 2 circulars. Unzip provisional CO sts and place them on spare needle. Beg knitting in rnd.

4 dpn	5 dpn	2 circular needles
With RS facing you, K6 (8, 10, 12, 14, 16, 18, 20, 22, 24) from needle A; cont with needle 1, PU and knit 2 sts from side edge. With needle 2, PU and knit 2 sts from side edge, K3 (4, 5, 6, 7, 8, 9, 10, 11, 12) from spare needle. With needle 3, K3 (4, 5, 6, 7, 8, 9, 10, 11, 12) from spare needle; PU and knit 2 sts from side edge. With last needle, PU and knit 2 sts from side edge, then knit rem sts from needle 1. Complete rnd by knitting across needles 2 and 3. Sts per needle: (10, 5, 5), (12, 6, 6), (14, 7, 7), (16, 8, 8), (18, 9, 9), (20, 10, 10), (22, 11, 11), (24, 12, 12), (26, 13, 13), (28, 14, 14)	With RS facing you, K3 (4, 5, 6, 7, 8, 9, 10, 11, 12) from needle A; these sts will be part of needle 1. With needle 2, K3 (4, 5, 6, 7, 8, 9, 10, 11, 12) from needle A, then PU and knit 2 sts from side edge. With needle 3, PU and knit 2 more sts from side edge, K3 (4, 5, 6, 7, 8, 9, 10, 11, 12) from spare needle. With needle 4, K3 (4, 5, 6, 7, 8, 9, 10, 11, 12) from spare needle, PU and knit 2 sts from side edge. With needle 5, PU and knit last 2 sts from side edge, knit first 3 sts; this is needle 1. Complete rnd by knitting across needles 2, 3, and 4. Sts per needle: 5 (6, 7, 8, 9, 10, 11, 12, 13, 14)	With RS facing you, K6 (8, 10, 12, 14, 16, 18, 20, 22, 24); cont with needle 1, PU and knit 2 sts from side edge. With needle 2, PU and knit 2 sts from side edge, K6 (8, 10, 12, 14, 16, 18, 20, 22, 24) from CO edge, PU and knit 2 sts from side edge. With needle 1, PU and knit 2 sts from side edge. Complete rnd by knitting across rem sts on needle 1 and across needle 2. Sts per needle: 10 (12, 14, 16, 18, 20, 22, 24, 26, 28)

Work toe incs as follows:

Rnd 1 Needle 1: K1, M1, knit to last st, M1, K1. Needle 2: K1, M1, knit to end. Needle 3: Knit to last st, M1, K1.	**Rnd 1** Needle 1: K1, M1, knit to end. Needle 2: Knit to last st, M1, K1. Needle 3: K1, M1, knit to end. Needle 4: Knit to last st, M1, K1.	**Rnd 1** Needle 1: K1, M1, knit to last st, M1, K1. Needle 2: K1, M1, knit to last st, M1, K1.

Rnd 2: Knit around.

Rep rnds 1 and 2 until 28 (40, 48, 60, 68, 80, 88, 100, 108, 120) total sts rem.

Note that if you are working a sock with 30, 50, 70, 90, or 110 sts for foot circumference, work rnd 3 as follows:

Rnd 3 Needle 1: Knit to last st, M1, K1. Needle 2: Knit 1, M1, knit to end. Needle 3: Knit.	**Rnd 3** Needle 1: Knit. Needle 2: Knit 1, M1, knit to end. Needle 3: Knit to last st, M1, K1. Needle 4: Knit.	**Rnd 3** Needle 1: Knit to last st, M1, K1. Needle 2: K1, M1, knit to end.

Rearrange sts by moving 1 st from sole to instep. This extra st on instep allows you to balance patt in instep. Work patt of choice on instep needle(s) until foot is desired length.

Needle 1: Instep sts Needles 2 and 3: Sole sts Sts per needle: (16, 5, 9), (21, 10, 9), (26, 10, 14), (31, 15, 14), (36, 15, 19), (41, 20, 19), (46, 20, 24), (51, 25, 24), (56, 25, 29), (61, 30, 29)	Needles 1 and 2: Instep sts Needles 3 and 4: Sole sts Sts per needle: (6, 10, 5, 9), (11, 10, 10, 9), (11, 15, 10, 14), (16, 15, 15, 14), (16, 20, 15, 19), (21, 20, 20, 19), (21, 25, 20, 24), (26, 25, 25, 24), (26, 30, 25, 29), (31, 30, 30, 29)	Needle 1: Instep sts Needle 2: Sole sts Sts per needle: (16, 14), (21, 19), (26, 24), (31, 29), (36, 34), (41, 39), (46, 44), (51, 49), (56, 54), (61, 59)
Combine sole sts onto needle 3, to become heel sts. Divide instep sts onto needles 1 and 2.	Combine sole sts onto needle 3, to become heel sts.	Sole sts are now heel sts.

HEEL

Work "Heel-Flap Heel" (page 23) or "Short-Row Heel" (page 24) on heel sts.

When you have completed heel and gusset or short-row heel, and 30 (40, 50, 60, 70, 80, 90, 100, 110, 120) total sts rem, rearrange sts as follows:

4 dpn	5 dpn	2 circular needles
(15, 5, 10), (20, 10, 10), (25, 10, 15), (30, 15, 15), (35, 15, 20), (40, 20, 20), (45, 20, 25), (50, 25, 25), (55, 25, 30), (60, 30, 30)	(5, 10, 5, 10), (10, 10, 10, 10), (10, 15, 10, 15), (15, 15, 15, 15), (15, 20, 15, 20), (20, 20, 20, 20), (20, 25, 20, 25), (25, 25, 25, 25), (25, 30, 25, 30), (30, 30, 30, 30)	15 (20, 25, 30, 35, 40, 45, 50, 55, 60)

LEG

Discontinue working extra st on instep patt and cont patt around leg to desired length.

CUFF

Work cuff for 1½" using suggested ribbing for leg patt you worked. BO loosely (page 77).

Six-Stitch Patterns with Even Instep and Heel Flap

As the width of a pattern increases, it has the potential to become more complex and texturally interesting. This collection of patterns offers a wide visual range from quite lacy to purely textural.

Crosshatch Lace sock made with Baby Ull from Dale of Norway (color 5726) on size 1 needle with a gauge of 8¾ sts to 1". This sock has a garter-edged, stockinette-stitch heel and a standard toe to highlight the lace pattern of the sock.

Double Lace Ribbing sock made with Meilenweit 6 fach from Lana Grossa (color 33 Cool Red) on size 2 needles with a gauge of 7¼ sts to 1". This sock starts at the toe with short-row toe shaping, has a short-row heel, and finishes with a frilled bind off.

Broad Spiral Ribbing sock made with Bearfoot from Mountain Colors (color Juniper) on size 2 needles with a gauge of 8 sts to 1". The sock has a heel-stitch heel with garter edge, and is finished with a standard toe, with the Broad Spiral Ribbing continuing to the tip.

MATERIALS

Gather materials for the socks you'd like to make and select the pattern you'd like to use.

DIRECTIONS

Select the number of sts to CO based on the gauge for your yarn and needles and the circumference of the intended foot.

SOCK STITCHES

Gauge sts/1"	Foot Circumference in Inches														
	5	5½	6	6½	7	7½	8	8½	9	9½	10	10½	11	11½	12
	Number of sts to CO														
5					36					48				60	60
5½				36				48	48			60	60		
6			36				48				60				72
6½		36				48			60	60			72	72	
7	36				48			60			72	72			84
7½				48			60			72			84	84	
8			48			60			72			84			96
8½		48			60			72			84		96	96	
9			60			72			84		96				108
9½	48					72			84		96			108	
10			60		72			84		96			108		120

TOP DOWN SOCK

CUFF AND LEG (FOR TOE-UP VERSION, SEE PAGE 31)

Using one of the COs beg on page 73, CO 36 (48, 60, 72, 84, 96, 108, 120) sts. Divide sts per needle as follows:

4 dpn	5 dpn	2 circular needles
(6, 12, 18), (12, 12, 24), (12, 18, 30), (18, 18, 36), (18, 24, 42), (24, 24, 48), (24, 30, 54), (30, 30, 60)	(6, 12, 6, 12), (12, 12, 12, 12), (12, 18, 12, 18), (18, 18, 18, 18), (18, 24, 18, 24), (24, 24, 24, 24), (24, 30, 24, 30), (30, 30, 30, 30)	18 (24, 30, 36, 42, 48, 54, 60)

Join, being careful not to twist sts. Work ribbing for 1½" using suggested ribbing for desired leg pattern (pages 90–92). Work leg to desired length.

HEEL

Work heel on 18 (24, 30, 36, 42, 48, 54, 60) sts, beg with WS row and ending with RS row.

Needles 1 and 2: Instep sts Needle 3: Heel sts Sts per needle: (6, 12, 18), (12, 12, 24), (12, 18, 30), (18, 18, 36), (18, 24, 42), (24, 24, 48), (24, 30, 54), (30, 30, 60)	Needles 1 and 2: Instep sts Combine sts on needles 3 and 4 onto needle 3, to become heel sts. Sts per needle: (6, 12, 18), (12, 12, 24), (12, 18, 30), (18, 18, 36), (18, 24, 42), (24, 24, 48), (24, 30, 54), (30, 30, 60)	Needle 1: Instep sts Needle 2: Heel sts Sts per needle: 18 (24, 30, 36, 42, 48, 54, 60)

You have a choice to work "Heel-Flap Heel" (page 29) or "Short-Row Heel" (page 30). If you are working heel-flap heel, cont working until you reach "Short-Row Heel," then skip to "Foot."

HEEL-FLAP HEEL

Work one of heel-st patts below or refer to "Heel Flaps" (page 66) for other options.

Turn work to beg heel on WS row.

Note that you will not sl sts at end of rows; you will work a garter selvage for picking up sts along heel flap.

St st with 3-st garter edge

Row 1 (WS): K3, purl to end.

Row 2: P3, knit to end.

Heel st with 3-st garter edge

Row 1 (WS): K3, purl to end.

Row 2: P3, *sl 1, K1, rep from * to last 3 sts, K3.

Rep rows 1 and 2 of selected heel-st patt until you have 18 (24, 30, 36, 42, 48, 54, 60) total rows in heel flap; last row should be a RS row.

HEEL TURN

Work as follows:

Row 1 (WS): Sl 1, P9 (12, 15, 18, 21, 24, 27, 30), P2tog, P1, turn.

Row 2: Sl 1, K3, ssk, K1, turn. Note that there will be a small gap between working sts that form heel turn and unworked heel sts.

Row 3: Sl 1, purl to within 1 st of gap, P2tog, P1, turn.

Row 4: Sl 1, knit to within 1 st of gap, ssk, K1, turn.

Rep rows 3 and 4, inc 1 additional knit or purl st after the sl 1 until all side sts are worked; end with completed row 4. There should be 12 (14, 16, 20, 24, 26, 30, 32) sts left on heel flap. When working rows 3 and 4, there may be no ending single st to work; some numbers don't work out.

For ease of instructions, beg of rnd is now at center of bottom of foot. The needles are renumbered at this point. Needle 1 is beg of rnd and holds all heel sts.

GUSSET

4 dpn	5 dpn	2 circular needles
Combine instep sts onto needle 2.	Needles 2 and 3: Instep sts	Needle 1: Heel sts Needle 2: Instep sts
With RS facing you and needle 1, PU and knit 9 (12, 15, 18, 21, 24, 27, 30) sts from side of heel flap, PU and knit 2 sts at top of gusset (see page 80).		
Needle 2: Work across instep in patt. Needle 3: PU and knit 2 sts at top of gusset, PU and knit 9 (12, 15, 18, 21, 24, 27, 30) sts from side of heel flap, K6 (7, 9, 10, 12, 13, 15, 16) from needle 1. Sts per needle: (17, 18, 17), (21, 24, 21), (24, 30, 24), (30, 36, 30), (35, 42, 35), (39, 48, 39), (44, 54, 44), (48, 60, 48)	Needles 2 and 3: Work across instep in patt. Needle 4: PU and knit 2 sts at top of gusset, PU and knit 9 (12, 15, 18, 21, 24, 27, 30) sts from side of heel flap, K6 (7, 9, 10, 12, 13, 15, 16) from needle 1. Sts per needle: (17, 6, 12, 17), (21, 12, 12, 21), (24, 12, 18, 24), (30, 18, 18, 30), (35, 18, 24, 35), (39, 24, 24, 39), (44, 24, 30, 44), (48, 30, 30, 48)	PM, work 12 (12, 18, 18, 24, 24, 30, 30) instep sts in patt. Needle 2: Work rem instep sts in patt, PM, PU and knit 2 sts at top of gusset, PU and knit 9 (12, 15, 18, 21, 24, 27, 30) sts from side of heel flap, K6 (7, 9, 10, 12, 13, 15, 16) from needle 1. The needles hold left half and right half of foot sts. Sts per needle: (29, 23), (33, 33), (42, 36), (48, 48), (59, 53), (63, 63), (74, 68), (78, 78)

CLOSE GUSSET TOP

Needle 1: Knit to last 2 sts, ssk. Needle 2: Work est patt. Needle 3: K2tog, knit to end.	Needle 1: Knit to last 2 sts, ssk. Needles 2 and 3: Work est patt. Needle 4: K2tog, knit to end.	Needle 1: Knit to 2 sts before marker, ssk, SM, work est patt to end. Needle 2: Work est patt to marker, SM, K2tog, knit to end.

GUSSET DECREASE

Rnd 1	Rnd 1	Rnd 1
Needle 1: Knit to last 3 sts, K2tog, K1. Needle 2: Work est patt. Needle 3: K1, ssk, knit to end.	Needle 1: Knit to last 3 sts, K2tog, K1. Needles 2 and 3: Work est patt. Needle 4: K1, ssk, knit to end.	Needle 1: Knit to 3 sts before marker, K2tog, K1, SM, work est patt. Needle 2: Work est patt to marker, SM, K1, ssk, knit to end.

Rnd 2: Work in est patt on instep, and in St st on sole.

Rep rnds 1 and 2 until 36 (48, 60, 72, 84, 96, 108, 120) total sts rem. Proceed to "Foot."

SHORT-ROW HEEL

Note that if you work heel sts on 2 needles, unworked sts are not stretched as much as if you use 1 needle. This also lessens the tendency to create gaps at base of heel.

Work heel back and forth on 18 (24, 30, 36, 42, 48, 54, 60) sts, foll instructions for "Short-Row Heel" on page 68. Rep rows 3 and 4 until 6 (8, 12, 14, 16, 18, 20, 22) sts rem unwrapped. End ready for a RS row.

Reverse short-row shaping.

With heel-st yarn, knit across heel, knitting wrap with last st of heel. Work across instep; when you get back to heel sts, knit first heel st with wrap.

FOOT

4 dpn	5 dpn	2 circular needles
Cont St st on needles 1 and 3, and est patt on needle 2 to desired heel-to-toe length.	Cont St st on needles 1 and 4, and est patt on needles 2 and 3 to desired heel-to-toe length.	Rearrange sts so instep sts are on needle 1, and sole sts are on needle 2. Markers are no longer needed. Cont est patt to desired heel-to-toe length.

TOE SHAPING

Adjust beg of rnd to side of foot as follows:

| Knit sts on needle 1.
Needle 1: Instep sts
Needles 2 and 3: Sole sts
Sts per needle: (18, 9, 9), (24, 12, 12), (30, 15, 15), (36, 18, 18), (42, 21, 21), (48, 24, 24), (54, 27, 27), (60, 30, 30) | Knit sts on needle 1.
Needles 1 and 2: Instep sts
Needles 3 and 4: Sole sts
Sts per needle: (12, 6, 9, 9), (12, 12, 12, 12), (18, 12, 15, 15), (18, 18, 18, 18), (24, 18, 21, 21), (24, 24, 24, 24), (30, 24, 27, 27), (30, 30, 30, 30) | Needle 1: Instep sts
Needle 2: Sole sts
Sts per needle: 18 (24, 30, 36, 42, 48, 54, 60) |

Work toe decs as follows:

Rnd 1	Rnd 1	Rnd 1
Needle 1: K1, ssk, work instep patt to last 3 sts, K2tog, K1. Needle 2: K1, ssk, knit to end. Needle 3: Knit to last 3 sts, K2tog, K1.	Needle 1: K1, ssk, work instep patt to end. Needle 2: Work instep patt to last 3 sts, K2tog, K1. Needle 3: K1, ssk, knit to end. Needle 4: Knit to last 3 sts, K2tog, K1.	Needle 1: K1, ssk, work instep patt to last 3 sts, K2tog, K1. Needle 2: K1, ssk, knit to last 3 sts, K2tog, K1.

Rnd 2: Knit around.

Rep rnds 1 and 2 until 20 (24, 32, 36, 44, 48, 56, 60) total sts rem. Sts for instep and sole are as follows: 10 (12, 16, 18, 22, 24, 28, 30).

Rep rnd 1 only until 12 (12, 16, 20, 24, 24, 28, 32) total sts rem. Sts for instep and sole are as follows: 6 (6, 8, 10, 12, 12, 14, 16).

Place instep sts on 1 needle and sole sts on 2nd needle. Graft sts tog with kitchener st (page 79).

TOE-UP INSTRUCTIONS

If you would like to work this sock from the toe up, follow these instructions for toe, and then follow instructions specifically for parts of the top-down sock as indicated.

SHORT-ROW TOE

Using waste yarn and provisional CO (page 76), CO 18 (24, 30, 36, 42, 48, 54, 60) sts. Purl 1 row with sock yarn. Remember to sl all sts purlwise.

Row 1 (RS): K17 (23, 29, 35, 41, 47, 53, 59), yf, sl next st, yb, PM, sl wrapped st back to LH needle, turn.

Row 2: P16 (22, 28, 34, 40, 46, 52, 58), yb, sl next st, yf, PM, sl wrapped st back to LH needle, turn.

Beg short-row shaping:

Row 3: Knit to st before last wrapped st, yf, sl next st, yb, PM, sl wrapped st back to LH needle, turn.

Row 4: Purl to st before last wrapped st, yb, sl next st, yf, PM, sl wrapped st back to LH needle, turn.

Rep rows 3 and 4 until 6 (8, 12, 14, 16, 18, 20, 22) sts rem unwrapped; end by working WS row.

Reverse short-row shaping:

Note: Your short rows will be more attractive if you sl the wrap up and over the st before knitting it tog with the st.

Row 1 (RS): Knit to next wrapped st (1 st before marker), knit this st tog with wrap, remove marker, yf, sl next st, yb, sl wrapped st back to LH needle, turn. This st now has 2 wraps.

Row 2: Purl to next wrapped st (1 st before marker), purl this st tog with wrap, drop marker, yb, sl next st to RH needle, yf, return st to LH needle. Turn.

Row 3: Knit to next wrapped st (1 st before marker), sl knit st to RH needle as if to purl, PU and knit wraps with LH needle and place on RH needle, sl all 3 sts back to LH needle as if to purl, K3tog, drop marker, yf, sl next st pwise, yb, sl st back to LH needle. Turn.

Row 4: Purl to next wrapped st (st before marker), sl purl st kwise, PU and knit 2 wraps from base of st and place on RH needle over first slipped st, sl them back one at a time pwise to LH needle, P3tog through back loops, drop marker, yb, sl next st pwise, yf, sl st back to LH needle. Turn.

Rep rows 3 and 4 until you have worked all double-wrapped sts and dropped all markers.

The 2 end sts have 1 wrap each. Beg knitting in rnd with RS facing you. K17 (23, 29, 35, 41, 47, 53, 59), knit next st tog with its wrap. PU and knit 18 (24, 30, 36, 42, 48, 54, 60) sts.

Arrange sts on needles as follows. This will allow you to have complete patts on each needle. Work patt of choice on instep sts, and St st on sole sts until foot is desired length.

4 dpn	5 dpn	2 circular needles
Needles 1 and 2: Sole sts	Needles 1 and 2: Sole sts	Needle 1: Sole sts
Needle 3: Inste	Needles 3 and 4: Instep sts	Needle 2: Instep sts
Sts per needle: (6, 12, 18), (12, 12, 24), (12, 18, 30), (18, 18, 36), (18, 24, 42), (24, 24, 48), (24, 30, 54), (30, 30, 60)	Sts per needle: (6, 12, 6, 12), (12, 12, 12, 12), (12, 18, 12, 18), (18, 18, 18, 18), (18, 24, 18, 24), (24, 24, 24, 24), (24, 30, 24, 30), (30, 30, 30, 30)	Sts per needle: 18 (24, 30, 36, 42, 48, 54, 60) Sole sts are now heel sts.
Combine sole sts onto needle 3, to become heel sts.	Combine sole sts onto needle 3, to become heel sts.	
Divide instep sts onto needles 1 and 2.		

HEEL

Work "Heel-Flap Heel" (page 29) or "Short-Row Heel" (page 30) on heel sts. When you have completed heel and gusset or short-row heel and 36 (48, 60, 72, 84, 96, 108, 120) sts rem, rearrange sts as follows:

(6, 12, 18), (12, 12, 24), (12, 18, 30), (18, 18, 36), (18, 24, 42), (24, 24, 48), (24, 30, 54), (30, 30, 60)	(6, 12, 6, 12), (12, 12, 12, 12), (12, 18, 12, 18), (18, 18, 18, 18), (18, 24, 18, 24), (24, 24, 24, 24), (24, 30, 24, 30), (30, 30, 30, 30)	18 (24, 30, 36, 42, 48, 54, 60)

LEG

Cont instep patt around leg to desired length.

CUFF

Work cuff for 1½" using suggested ribbing for leg patt you worked. BO loosely (page 77).

Six-Stitch Patterns with Uneven Instep and Heel Flap

This set of patterns also has six-stitch repeats, but they need an additional stitch to balance them on the instep. As the patterns get wider, there is more variety of texture, from simple knit-and-purl decorations to lace and interesting ribs.

SKILL LEVEL: EASY ◼◼◻◻

Hourglass Eyelets sock made with Essential from Knit Picks (color 23699 Pumpkin) on size 1 needles with a gauge of 8¾ sts to 1". This sock starts at the top, then is worked with a garter-edged, heel-stitch heel and a standard toe.

Small Tiles sock made with Weaver's Wool Quarters from Mountain Colors (color Steelhead) on size 2 needles with a gauge of 8 sts to 1". This sock starts at the top, has a heel knit with a chain selvage in heel stitch, and has a standard toe adorned with the instep pattern.

Shirred Ribbing sock made with Shepherd Sport from Lorna's Laces (color 23ns Berry) on size 2 needles with a gauge of 7¾ sts to 1". This toe-up sock is worked with a stockinette-stitch heel flap on the sole, then heel stitch is worked on the heel turn and continued on the back of the heel for added durability. A picot stitch gives a loose bind off with style.

MATERIALS

Gather materials for the socks you'd like to make and select the pattern you'd like to use.

DIRECTIONS

Select the number of sts to CO based on the gauge for your yarn and needles and the circumference of the intended foot.

SOCK STITCHES

Gauge sts/1"	Foot Circumference in Inches														
	5	5½	6	6½	7	7½	8	8½	9	9½	10	10½	11	11½	12
	Number of sts to CO														
5					36					48	48			60	60
5½				36			48	48				60	60		
6			36			48					60				72
6½		36			48			60	60				72	72	
7	36				48		60				72	72			84
7½			48			60				72			84	84	
8		48			60			72				84			96
8½	48			60			72				84		96	96	
9			60			72			84			96			108
9½	48					72		84			96			108	
10			60		72			84		96			108		120

TOP-DOWN SOCK

CUFF AND LEG (FOR TOE-UP VERSION, SEE PAGE 35)

Using one of the COs beg on page 73, CO 36 (48, 60, 72, 84, 96, 108, 120) sts. Divide sts per needle as follows:

4 dpn	5 dpn	2 circular needles
(6, 12, 18), (12, 12, 24), (12, 18, 30), (18, 18, 36), (18, 24, 42), (24, 24, 48), (24, 30, 54), (30, 30, 60)	(6, 12, 6, 12), (12, 12, 12, 12), (12, 18, 12, 18), (18, 18, 18, 18), (18, 24, 18, 24), (24, 24, 24, 24), (24, 30, 24, 30), (30, 30, 30, 30)	18 (24, 30, 36, 42, 48, 54, 60)

Join, being careful not to twist sts. Work ribbing for 1½" using suggested ribbing for desired leg pattern (pages 93–94). Work leg to desired length.

HEEL

Work heel on 17 (23, 29, 35, 41, 47, 53, 59) sts, beg with WS row and ending with RS row. Move 1 st from heel to instep as follows to balance patt on instep:

Unwork last st on needle 3 and place it on needle 1. Needles 1 and 2: Instep sts Needle 3: Heel sts	Unwork last st on needle 4 and place it on needle 1. Sl all sts from needle 4 to needle 3. Needles 1 and 2: Instep sts Needle 3: Heel sts.	Unwork last st on needle 2 and place it on needle 1. Needle 1: Instep sts Needle 2: Heel sts

You have a choice to work "Heel-Flap Heel" (page 34) or "Short-Row Heel" (page 35). If you are working heel-flap heel, cont working until you reach "Short-Row Heel," then skip to "Foot."

HEEL-FLAP HEEL

Work one of heel-st patts below or refer to "Heel Flaps" (page 66) for other options.

Turn work to beg heel on WS row.

Heel st with chain selvage

Sl *last* st of row, not first; this makes a neater chain to pick up into rather than first st.

Row 1 (WS): K1, purl to last st, sl 1 wyif.

Row 2: K1, *sl 1 wyib, K1, rep from * to last 2 sts, sl 1 wyib, sl 1 wyif.

Note that you will not sl sts at end of row in foll heel-st patts; you will create a garter-edge selvage for picking up sts along heel flap.

Heel st with 3-st garter edge

Row 1 (WS): K3, purl to end.

Row 2: P3, *sl 1 wyib, K1, rep from * to last 4 sts, sl 1, K3.

St st with 3-st garter edge

Row 1 (WS): K3, purl to end.

Row 2: P3, knit to end.

Rep rows 1 and 2 of selected heel-st patt until you have 18 (24, 30, 36, 42, 48, 54, 60) total rows in heel flap; last row should be RS row.

HEEL TURN

Work as follows:

If you worked a chain-selvage edge on heel flap, purl first stitch; do not slip it twice.

Row 1 (WS): Sl 1, P9 (12, 15, 18, 21, 24, 27, 30), P2tog, P1, turn.

Row 2: Sl 1, K4, ssk, K1, turn. Note that there will be a small gap between working sts that form heel turn and unworked heel sts.

Row 3: Sl 1, purl to within 1 st of gap, P2tog, P1, turn.

Row 4: Sl 1, knit to within 1 st of gap, ssk, K1, turn.

Rep rows 3 and 4, inc 1 additional knit or purl st after the sl 1 until all side sts are worked; end with completed row 4. There should be 11 (13, 17, 19, 23, 25, 29, 31) sts left on heel flap. When working rows 3 and 4, there may be no ending single st to work; some numbers don't work out.

For ease of instructions, beg of rnd is now at center of bottom of foot. The needles are renumbered at this point. Needle 1 is beg of rnd and holds all heel-turn sts.

GUSSET

4 dpn	5 dpn	2 circular needles
Combine instep sts onto needle 2.	Needles 2 and 3: Instep sts	Needle 1: Heel sts Needle 2: Instep sts
With RS facing you and needle 1, PU and knit 9 (12, 15, 18, 21, 24, 27, 30) sts from side of heel flap, PU and knit 2 sts at top of gusset (see page 80), then		
Needle 2: Work across instep in patt. Needle 3: PU and knit 2 sts at top of gusset, PU and knit 9 (12, 15, 18, 21, 24, 27, 30) sts from side of heel flap, K5 (6, 8, 9, 11, 12, 14, 15) from needle 1. Sts per needle: (17, 19, 16), (21, 25, 20), (26, 31, 25), (30, 37, 29), (35, 43, 34), (39, 49, 38), (44, 55, 43), (48, 61, 47)	Needles 2 and 3: Work across instep in patt. Needle 4: PU and knit 2 sts at top of gusset, PU and knit 9 (12, 15, 18, 21, 24, 27, 30) sts from side of heel flap, K5 (6, 8, 9, 11, 12, 14, 15) from needle 1. Sts per needle: (17, 13, 6, 16), (21, 13, 12, 20), (26, 19, 12, 25), (30, 19, 18, 29), (35, 25, 18, 34), (39, 25, 24, 38), (44, 31, 24, 43), (48, 31, 30, 47)	PM, work 13 (13, 19, 19, 25, 25, 31, 31) instep sts in patt. Needle 2: Work rem of instep sts in patt, PM, PU and knit 2 sts at top of gusset, PU and knit 9 (12, 15, 18, 21, 24, 27, 30) sts from side of heel flap, K5 (6, 8, 9, 11, 12, 14, 15) from needle 1. The needles hold left half and right half of foot sts rather than sts for instep and bottom of foot. Sts per needle: (30, 22), (34, 32), (45, 37), (49, 47), (60, 52), (64, 62), (75, 67), (79, 77)

CLOSE GUSSET TOP

Needle 1: Knit to last 2 sts, ssk. Needle 2: Work est patt. Needle 3: K2tog, knit to end.	Needle 1: Knit to last 2 sts, ssk. Needles 2 and 3: Work est patt. Needle 4: K2tog, knit to end.	Needle 1: Knit to 2 sts before marker, ssk, SM, work est patt to end. Needle 2: Work est patt to marker, SM, K2tog, knit to end.

GUSSET DECREASE

Rnd 1	Rnd 1	Rnd 1
Needle 1: Knit to last 3 sts, K2tog, K1. Needle 2: Work est patt. Needle 3: K1, ssk, knit to end.	Needle 1: Knit to last 3 sts, K2tog, K1. Needles 2 and 3: Work est patt. Needle 4: K1, ssk, knit to end.	Needle 1: Knit to 3 sts before marker, K2tog, K1, SM, work est patt. Needle 2: Work est patt to marker, SM, K1, ssk, knit to end.

Rnd 2: Work est patt on instep sts and St st on sole sts.

Rep rnds 1 and 2 until 36 (48, 60, 72, 84, 96, 108, 120) total sts rem. Proceed to "Foot."

SHORT-ROW HEEL

Note that if you work heel sts on 2 needles, unworked sts are not stretched as much as if you use 1 needle. This also lessens the tendency to create gaps at base of heel.

Work heel back and forth on 17 (23, 29, 35, 41, 47, 53, 59) sts, foll instructions for "Short-Row Heel" on page 68. Rep rows 3 and 4 until 5 (7, 11, 13, 15, 17, 19, 21) sts rem unwrapped. End ready for a RS row.

Reverse short-row shaping.

With heel-st yarn, knit across heel, knitting wrap with last st of heel. Work across instep; when you get back to heel sts, knit first heel st with wrap.

FOOT

4 dpn	5 dpn	2 circular needles
Cont St st on needles 1 and 3, and est patt on needle 2 to desired heel-to-toe length.	Cont St st on needles 1 and 4, and est patt on needles 2 and 3 to desired heel-to-toe length.	Rearrange sts so instep sts are on needle 1, and sole sts are on needle 2. Markers are no longer needed. Cont est patt to desired heel-to-toe length.

TOE SHAPING: STANDARD TOE

Adjust beg of rnd to side of foot as follows:

Knit sts on needle 1. Needle 1: Instep sts Needles 2 and 3: Sole sts Sts per needle: (19, 8, 9), (25, 11, 12), (31, 14, 15), (37, 17, 18), (43, 20, 21), (49, 23, 24), (55, 26, 27), (61, 29, 30)	Knit sts on needle 1. Needles 1 and 2: Instep sts Needles 3 and 4: Sole sts Sts per needle: (13, 6, 8, 9), (13, 12, 11, 12), (19, 12, 14, 15), (19, 18, 17, 18), (25, 18, 20, 21), (25, 24, 23, 24), (31, 24, 26, 27), (31, 30, 29, 30)	Needle 1: Instep sts Needle 2: Sole sts Sts per needle: (19, 17), (25, 23), (31, 29), (37, 35), (43, 41), (49, 47), (55, 53), (61, 59)

Work toe decs as follows:

Rnd 1	Rnd 1	Rnd 1
Needle 1: K1, ssk, work instep patt to last 3 sts, K2tog, K1. Needle 2: K1, ssk, knit to end. Needle 3: Knit to last 3 sts, K2tog, K1.	Needle 1: K1, ssk, work instep patt to end. Needle 2: Work instep patt to last 3 sts, K2tog, K1. Needle 3: K1, ssk, knit to end. Needle 4: Knit to last 3 sts, K2tog, K1.	Needle 1: K1, ssk, work instep patt to last 3 sts, K2tog, K1. Needle 2: K1, ssk, knit to last 3 sts, K2tog, K1.

Rnd 2: Knit around.

Rep rnds 1 and 2 until 20 (24, 32, 36, 44, 48, 56, 60) total sts rem. Sts for instep and sole: (11, 9), (13, 11), (17, 15), (19, 17), (23, 21), (25, 23), (29, 27), (31, 29).

Rep rnd 1 only until 10 (10, 14, 18, 22, 22, 26, 30) total sts rem. There are 5 (5, 7, 9, 11, 11, 13, 15) sts each on instep and sole; last 2 dec will be on instep.

Place instep sts on 1 needle and sole sts on 2nd needle. Graft sts tog with kitchener st (page 79).

TOE-UP SOCKS

If you would like to work this sock from the toe up, follow these instructions for toe, and then follow instructions specifically for parts of top-down socks as indicated.

EASY TOE

With waste yarn and provisional CO (see page 76), CO 8 (10, 12, 14, 16, 20, 22, 24) sts. Purl 1 row with sock yarn.

Work back and forth in St st for 6 rows or until rectangle is approx ½" high; end on a purl row, call the needle with these sts needle A for 4 dpn and 5 dpn, and needle 1 for 2 circulars. Unzip provisional CO sts and place them on spare needle. Beg knitting in rnd.

4 dpn	5 dpn	2 circular needles
With RS facing you, K8 (10, 12, 14, 16, 20, 22, 24) from needle A; cont with needle 1, PU and knit 2 sts from side edge. With needle 2, PU and knit 2 sts from side edge, K4 (5, 6, 7, 8, 10, 11, 12) from spare needle. With needle 3, K4 (5, 6, 7, 8, 10, 11, 12) from spare needle, then PU and knit 2 sts from side edge. With last needle, PU and knit 2 sts from side edge, then knit rem sts from needle 1. Complete rnd by knitting across needles 2 and 3. Sts per needle: (12, 6, 6), (14, 7, 7), (16, 8, 8), (18, 9, 9), (20, 10, 10), (24, 12, 12), (26, 13, 13), (28, 14, 14)	With RS facing you, K4 (5, 6, 7, 8, 10, 11, 12) from needle A; these sts will be part of needle 1. With needle 2, K4 (5, 6, 7, 8, 10, 11, 12) from needle A, then PU and knit 2 sts from side edge. With needle 3, PU and knit 2 more sts from side edge, K4 (5, 6, 7, 8, 10, 11, 12) from spare needle. With needle 4, K4 (5, 6, 7, 8, 10, 11, 12) from spare needle, then PU and knit 2 sts from side edge. With needle 5, PU and knit last 2 sts from side edge, knit first 6 sts; this is needle 1. Complete rnd by knitting across needles 2, 3, and 4. Sts per needle: 6 (7, 8, 9, 10, 12, 13, 14)	With RS facing you, K8 (10, 12, 14, 16, 20, 22, 24); cont with needle 1, PU and knit 2 sts from side edge. With needle 2, PU and knit 2 sts from side edge, K8 (10, 12, 14, 16, 20, 22, 24) from CO edge, PU and knit 2 sts from side edge. With needle 1, PU and knit 2 sts from side edge. Complete rnd by knitting across rem sts on needle 1 and across needle 2. Sts per needle: 12 (14, 16, 18, 20, 24, 26, 28)

Work toe incs as follows:

Rnd 1 Needle 1: K1, M1, knit to last st, M1, K1. Needle 2: K1, M1, knit to end. Needle 3: Knit to last st, M1, K1.	**Rnd 1** Needle 1: K1, M1, knit to end. Needle 2: Knit to last st, M1, K1. Needle 3: K1, M1, knit to end. Needle 4: Knit to last st, M1, K1.	**Rnd 1** Needle 1: K1, M1, knit to last st, M1, K1. Needle 2: K1, M1, knit to last st, M1, K1.

Rnd 2: Knit around.

Rep rnds 1 and 2 until 36 (48, 60, 72, 84, 96, 108, 120) total sts rem.

Rearrange sts by moving 1 st from sole to instep. This extra st on instep allows you to balance patt in instep.

Work patt of choice on instep sts until foot is desired length.

Needle 1: Instep sts Needles 2 and 3: Sole sts Sts per needle: (19, 9, 8), (25, 12, 11), (31, 15, 14), (37, 18, 17), (43, 21, 20), (49, 24, 23), (55, 27, 26), (61, 30, 29) Combine sole sts onto needle 3, to become heel sts. Divide instep sts onto needles 1 and 2.	Needles 1 and 2: Instep sts Needles 3 and 4: Sole sts Sts per needle: (7, 12, 9, 8), (13, 12, 12, 11), (13, 18, 15, 14), (19, 18, 18, 17), (19, 24, 21, 20), (25, 24, 24, 23), (25, 30, 27, 26), (31, 30, 30, 29) Combine sole sts onto needle 3, to become heel sts.	Needle 1: Instep sts Needle 2: Sole sts Sts per needle: (19, 17), (25, 23), (31, 29), (37, 35), (43, 41), (49, 47), (55, 53), (61, 59) Sole sts are now heel sts.

HEEL

Work "Heel-Flap Heel" (page 34) on heel sts.

When you have completed heel flap and 36 (48, 60, 72, 84, 96, 108, 120) total sts rem, rearrange sts as follows:

(6, 12, 18), (12, 12, 24), (12, 18, 30), (18, 18, 36), (18, 24, 42), (24, 24, 48), (24, 30, 54), (30, 30, 60)	(6, 12, 6, 12), (12, 12, 12, 12), (12, 18, 12, 18), (18, 18, 18, 18), (18, 24, 18, 24), (24, 24, 24, 24), (24, 30, 24, 30), (30, 30, 30, 30)	18 (24, 30, 36, 42, 48, 54, 60)

LEG

Discontinue working extra st on instep patt and cont patt around leg to desired length.

CUFF

Work cuff for 1½" using suggested ribbing for leg patt you worked. BO loosely (page 77).

EIGHT-STITCH PATTERNS

The three patterns knit as samples all have an interesting structure of separated increases and decreases at the beginning of the pattern. This separation is closed during the working of the pattern, causing the fabric to pull off center and have a biased appearance. They are among my favorite patterns as they are visually so interesting. Because of the biased nature of the fabric, the socks tend to stretch less than a ribbed pattern would, so you may need to use a larger needle on the leg or calculate your foot size a bit larger.

SKILL LEVEL: INTERMEDIATE ◖■■■◗

Traveling Vine sock made with Gems Merino Opal from Louet Sales (color 48 Aqua) on size 2 needles with a gauge of 6¾ sts to 1". Twice as many stitches are cast on and then decreased to the desired number in the first round, then all the knit stitches are twisted as they are knit. The eye-of-partridge heel is edged with seed stitch, and the sock is finished with a round toe.

Scrolls sock made with hand-spun Coopworth and alpaca (dyed with Lanaset Scarlet) on size 1 needles with a gauge of 8 sts to 1". A garter-edged stockinette heel and a standard toe are calm enough to show off the scrolls pattern.

Milanese Lace sock made with Twist of Fate sock yarn (dyed with Lanaset 50% Blue, 50% Turquoise) on size 3 needles with a gauge of 6½ sts to 1". Started with an easy toe and worked with a short-row heel, the sock is finished with K2, P2 ribbing and bound off with kitchener stitch for a beautiful and stretchy edge.

MATERIALS

Gather materials for the socks you'd like to make and select the pattern you'd like to use.

DIRECTIONS

Select the number of sts to CO based on the gauge for your yarn and needles and the circumference of the intended foot.

SOCK STITCHES

Foot Circumference in Inches / Number of sts to CO

Gauge sts/1"	5	5½	6	6½	7	7½	8	8½	9	9½	10	10½	11	11½	12
5				32						48					64
5½			32					48	48					64	
6		32					48					64	64		
6½	32					48				64	64				80
7					48				64				80	80	
7½				48				64				80			
8			48				64				80				96
8½		48				64				80			96	96	
9		48			64				80			96			
9½	48			64				80			96			112	112
10				64			80			96			112		

TOP-DOWN SOCK

CUFF AND LEG (FOR TOE-UP VERSION, SEE PAGE 41)

Using one of the COs beg on page 73, CO 32 (48, 64, 80, 96, 112) sts. Divide sts per needle as follows:

4 dpn	5 dpn	2 circular needles
(8, 8, 16), (16, 8, 24), (16, 16, 32), (24, 16, 40), (24, 24, 48), (32, 24, 56)	(8, 8, 8, 8), (16, 8, 16, 8), (16, 16, 16, 16), (24, 16, 24, 16), (24, 24, 24, 24), (32, 24, 32, 24)	16 (24, 32, 40, 48, 56)

Join, being careful not to twist sts. Work ribbing for 1½" using suggested ribbing for desired leg pattern (pages 95–97). Work leg to desired length.

HEEL

Work heel on 16 (24, 32, 40, 48, 56) sts, beg with WS row and ending with RS row.

Work heel on needle 3.	Sl sts from needle 4 to needle 3 to work on heel flap. Set needle 4 aside. Work heel on needle 3.	

Sts per needle:

Needles 1 and 2: Instep sts Needle 3: Heel sts Sts per needle: (8, 8, 16), (16, 8, 24), (16, 16, 32), (24, 16, 40), (24, 24, 48), (32, 24, 56)	Needles 1 and 2: Instep sts Combine sts on needles 3 and 4 on needle 3 to become heel sts. Sts per needle: (8, 8, 16), (16, 8, 24), (16, 16, 32), (24, 16, 40), (24, 24, 48), (32, 24, 56)	Needle 1: Instep sts Needle 2: Heel sts Sts per needle: 16 (24, 32, 40, 48, 56)

You have a choice to work "Heel-Flap Heel" (page 39) or "Short-Row Heel" (page 40). If you are working heel-flap heel, cont working until you reach "Short-Row Heel," then skip to "Foot."

HEEL-FLAP HEEL

Work one of heel-st patts below or refer to "Heel Flaps" (page 66) for other options.

Turn work to beg heel on WS row.

Eye-of-partridge heel with seed-st edging

Rows 1 and 3 (WS): K1, P1, K1, purl to last 3 sts, K1, P1, K1.

Row 2: K1, P1, K1, *K1, sl 1, rep from * to last 3 sts, K1, P1, K1.

Row 4: K1, P1, K1, *sl 1, K1, rep from * to last 3 sts, K1, P1, K1.

Rep rows 1–4 until you have 16 (24, 32, 40, 48, 56) heel-flap rows; last row should be RS row.

Heel st with 3-st garter edge

Row 1 (WS): K3, purl to end.

Row 2: P3, *K1, sl 1, rep from * to last 4 sts, K4.

Rep rows 1 and 2 until you have 16 (24, 32, 40, 48, 56) heel-flap rows; last row should be RS row.

HEEL TURN

Work as follows:

Row 1 (WS): Sl 1, P8 (12, 16, 20, 24, 28) sts, P2tog, P1, turn.

Row 2: Sl 1, K3, ssk, K1, turn. Note that there will be a small gap between working sts that form heel turn and unworked heel sts.

Row 3: Sl 1, purl to within 1 st of gap, P2tog (1 st on either side of gap), P1, turn.

Row 4: Sl 1, knit to within 1 st of gap, ssk, K1, turn.

Rep rows 3 and 4, inc 1 additional knit or purl st after sl 1 until all side sts are worked, end with RS row. There are 10 (14, 18, 22, 26, 30) sts left on heel flap.

For ease of instructions, beg of rnd is now at center of bottom of foot. The needles are renumbered at this point. Needle 1 is beg of rnd and holds all heel-turn sts.

GUSSET

4 dpn	5 dpn	2 circular needles
Combine instep sts onto needle 2.	Needles 2 and 3: Instep sts	Needle 1: Heel sts Needle 2: Instep sts

With RS facing you and needle 1, PU and knit 8 (12, 16, 20, 24, 28) sts from side of heel flap, PU and knit 2 sts at top of gusset (see page 80).

Needle 2: Work across instep in est patt. Needle 3: PU and knit 2 sts at top of gusset, PU and knit 8 (12, 16, 20, 24, 28) sts from side of heel flap, K5 (7, 9, 11, 13, 15) from needle 1. Sts per needle: (15, 16, 15), (21, 24, 21), (27, 32, 27), (33, 40, 33), (39, 48, 39), (45, 56, 45)	Needles 2 and 3: Work across instep in est patt. Needle 4: PU and knit 2 sts at top of gusset, PU and knit 8 (12, 16, 20, 24, 28) sts from side of heel flap, K5 (7, 9, 11, 13, 15) from needle 1. Sts per needle: (15, 8, 8, 15), (21, 16, 8, 21), (27, 16, 16, 27), (33, 24, 16, 33), (39, 24, 24, 39), (45, 32, 24, 45)	Cont with needle 1, PM, K8 (8, 16, 16, 24, 24) instep sts from needle 2. Needle 2: Work rem of instep sts, PM, PU and knit 2 sts at top of gusset, PU and knit 8 (12, 16, 20, 24, 28) sts from side of heel flap, K5 (7, 9, 11, 13, 15) from needle 1. Sts per needle: (23, 23), (37, 29), (43, 43), (57, 49), (63, 63), (77, 69) Needles now hold left and right sides of sock.

CLOSE GUSSET TOP

Needle 1: Knit to last 2 sts, ssk. Needle 2: Work est patt. Needle 3: K2tog, knit to end.	Needle 1: Knit to last 2 sts, ssk. Needles 2 and 3: Work est patt. Needle 4: K2tog, knit to end.	Needle 1: Knit to 2 sts before marker, ssk, SM, work est patt to end. Needle 2: Work est patt to marker, SM, K2tog, knit to end.

GUSSET DECREASE

Rnd 1	Rnd 1	Rnd 1
Needle 1: Knit to last 3 sts, K2tog, K1. Needle 2: Work est patt. Needle 3: K1, ssk, knit to end.	Needle 1: Knit to last 3 sts, K2tog, K1. Needles 2 and 3: Work est patt. Needle 4: K1, ssk, knit to end.	Needle 1: Knit to 3 sts before marker, K2tog, K1, SM, work est patt. Needle 2: Work est patt to marker, SM, K1, ssk, knit to end.

Rnd 2: Work in est patt on instep sts, and in St st on sole sts.

Rep rnds 1 and 2 until 32 (48, 64, 80, 96, 112) total sts rem.

Proceed to "Foot."

SHORT-ROW HEEL

Note that if you work heel sts on 2 needles, unworked sts are not stretched as much as if you use 1 needle. This also lessens the tendency to create gaps at base of heel.

Work heel back and forth on 16 (24, 32, 40, 48, 56) sts, foll instructions for "Short-Row Heel" on page 68. Rep rows 3 and 4 until 6 (10, 14, 16, 20, 24) sts rem unwrapped. End ready for a RS row.

Reverse short-row shaping.

The heel is now finished, and you have both end sts wrapped. With heel-st yarn, knit across heel, knitting wrap with last st of heel. Work across instep; when you get back to heel sts, knit first heel st with wrap.

FOOT

4 dpn	5 dpn	2 circular needles
Sts per needle: (8, 16, 8), (12, 24, 12), (16, 32, 16), (20, 40, 20), (24, 48, 24), (28, 56, 28) Cont St st on needles 1 and 3, and est patt on needle 2 to desired heel-to-toe length.	Sts per needle: 8 (12, 16, 20, 24, 28) Cont St st on needles 1 and 4, and est patt on needles 2 and 3 to desired heel-to-toe length.	Rearrange sts so that instep sts are on needle 1 and sole sts are on needle 2. Sts per needle: 16 (24, 32, 40, 48, 56) Cont est patt on needle 1, and St st on needle 2 to desired heel-to-toe length.

TOE SHAPING

| Knit sts on needle 1.
Renumber needles.
Needle 1: Instep sts
Needles 2 and 3: Sole sts
Sts per needle: (16, 8, 8), (24, 12, 12), (32, 16, 16), (40, 20, 20), (48, 24, 24), (56, 28, 28) | Knit sts on needle 1.
Renumber needles.
Needles 1 and 2: Instep sts
Needles 3 and 4: Sole sts
Sts per needle: 8 (12, 16, 20, 24, 28) | Needle 1: Instep sts
Needle 2: Sole sts
Sts per needle: 16 (24, 32, 40, 48, 56) |

Work toe decs as follows:

Rnd 1	**Rnd 1**	**Rnd 1**
Needle 1: K1, ssk, knit to last 3 sts, K2tog, K1. Needle 2: K1, ssk, knit to end. Needle 3: Knit to last 3 sts, K2tog, K1.	Needle 1: K1, ssk, knit to end. Needle 2: Knit to last 3 sts, K2tog, K1. Needle 3: K1, ssk, knit to end. Needle 4: Knit to last 3 sts, K2tog, K1.	Needle 1: K1, ssk, knit to last 3 sts, K2tog, K1. Needle 2: K1, ssk, knit to last 3 sts, K2tog, K1.

Rnd 2: Knit around.

Rep rnds 1 and 2 until 16 (24, 32, 40, 48, 56) total sts rem. Sts for instep and sole are as follows: 8 (12, 16, 20, 24, 28).

Rep rnd 1 only until 8 (12, 16, 20, 24, 28) total sts rem. Sts for instep and sole are as follows: 4 (6, 8, 10, 12, 14).

Place instep sts on 1 needle, and sole sts on 2nd needle. Graft sts tog with kitchener st (page 79).

TOE-UP INSTRUCTIONS

If you would like to work this sock from the toe up, follow these instructions for toe, and then follow instructions specifically for parts of top-down socks as indicated.

EASY TOE

With waste yarn and provisional CO (see page 76), CO 6 (10, 12, 16, 20, 22) sts. Purl 1 row with sock yarn. Work back and forth in St st for 6 rows or until rectangle is approx ½" high; end on a purl row, call the needle with these sts needle A for 4 dpn and 5 dpn, and needle 1 for 2 circulars. Unzip provisional CO sts and place them on spare needle. Beg knitting in rnd.

4 dpn	5 dpn	2 circular needles
With RS facing you, K6 (10, 12, 16, 20, 22) from needle A; cont with needle 1, PU and knit 2 sts from side edge. With needle 2, PU and knit 2 sts from side edge, K3 (5, 6, 8, 10, 11) from spare needle. With needle 3, K3 (5, 6, 8, 10, 11) from spare needle, then PU and knit 2 sts from side edge. With last needle, PU and knit 2 sts from side edge, then knit rem sts from needle 1. Complete rnd by knitting across needles 2 and 3. Sts per needle: (10, 5, 5), (14, 7, 7), (16, 8, 8), (20, 10, 10), (24, 12, 12), (26, 13, 13)	With RS facing you, K3 (5, 6, 8, 10, 11) from needle A; these sts will be part of needle 1. With needle 2, K3 (5, 6, 8, 10, 11) from needle A, then PU and knit 2 sts from side edge. With needle 3, PU and knit 2 sts from side edge, K3 (5, 6, 8, 10, 11) from spare needle. With needle 4, K3 (5, 6, 8, 10, 11) from spare needle, then PU and knit 2 sts from side edge. With needle 5, PU and knit last 2 sts from side edge, knit first 3 (5, 6, 8, 10, 11) sts; this is needle 1. Complete rnd by knitting across needles 2, 3, and 4. Sts per needle: 5 (7, 8, 10, 12, 13)	With RS facing you, K6 (10, 12, 16, 20, 22); cont with needle 1, PU and knit 2 sts from side edge. With needle 2, PU and knit 2 sts from side edge, K6 (10, 12, 16, 20, 22) from CO edge, PU and knit 2 sts from side edge. With needle 1, PU and knit 2 sts from side edge. Complete rnd by knitting across rem sts on needle 1 and across needle 2. Sts per needle: 10 (14, 16, 20, 24, 26)

Work toe incs as follows:

Rnd 1	Rnd 1	Rnd 1
Needle 1: K1, M1, knit to last st, M1, K1. Needle 2: K1, M1, knit to end. Needle 3: Knit to last st, M1, K1.	Needle 1: K1, M1, knit to end. Needle 2: Knit to last st, M1, K1. Needle 3: K1, M1, knit to end. Needle 4: Knit to last st, M1, K1.	Needle 1: K1, M1, knit to last st, M1, K1. Needle 2: K1, M1, knit to last st, M1, K1.

Rnd 2: Knit around.

Rep rnds 1 and 2 until 32 (48, 64, 80, 96, 112) total sts rem.

Needle 1: Instep sts Needles 2 and 3: Sole sts Sts per needle: (16, 8, 8), (24, 12, 12), (32, 16, 16), (40, 20, 20), (48, 24, 24), (56, 28, 28)	Needles 1 and 2: Instep sts Needles 3 and 4: Sole sts Sts per needle: 8 (12, 16, 20, 24, 28)	Needle 1: Instep sts Needle 2: Sole sts Sts per needle: 16 (24, 32, 40, 48, 56)

Work patt of choice on instep sts until foot is desired length.

Combine sole sts onto needle 3, to become heel sts. Divide instep sts onto needles 1 and 2.	Combine sole sts onto needle 3, to become heel sts.	Sole sts are now heel sts.

HEEL

Work "Heel-Flap Heel" (page 39) or "Short-Row Heel" (page 40) on heel sts. When you have completed heel and gusset or short-row heel and 32 (48, 64, 80, 96, 112) total sts rem, rearrange sts as follows:

(8, 8, 16), (12, 12, 24), (16, 16, 32), (20, 20, 40), (24, 24, 48), (28, 28, 56)	8 (12, 16, 20, 24, 28)	16 (24, 32, 40, 48, 56)

LEG

Cont instep patt around leg to desired length.

CUFF

Work cuff for 1½" using suggested ribbing for leg patt you worked. BO loosely (page 77).

TEN-STITCH PATTERNS

There is a nice variety of lace as well as ribbed and textured patterns to work. There are some more complex and difficult patterns, but some are just beautiful knit and purl combinations.

SKILL LEVEL: INTERMEDIATE ◼◼◼▢

Leafy Lace sock made with Sock! from Lisa Souza (color Foxglove) on size 1 needle with a gauge of 9 sts to 1". Starting with a round toe, the sock is worked with a garter-edged stockinette-stitch heel flap on the sole of the heel, and stockinette stitch on the entire gusset. It is finished with a picot bind off for decoration as well as looseness at the top.

Waffle Stitch sock made with Shepherd Sport from Lorna's Laces (color 40ns Sunshine) on size 2 needles with a gauge of 8 sts to 1". Started at the top, this sock has a garter-edged heel flap made with heel stitch and a standard toe, with waffle stitch continuing all the way to the tip.

Garter Ribbing sock made with Shepherd Sport from Lorna's Laces (color 51ns Island Blue) on size 2 needles with a gauge of 8 sts to 1". Started at the top, this sock has a heel-stitched heel flap worked with a chain selvage, and finishes with a standard toe. The garter ribbing continues all the way to the end.

MATERIALS

Gather materials for the socks you'd like to make and select the pattern you'd like to use.

DIRECTIONS

Select the number of sts to CO based on the gauge for your yarn and needles and the circumference of the intended foot.

SOCK STITCHES

Gauge sts/1"	Foot Circumference in Inches														
	5	5½	6	6½	7	7½	8	8½	9	9½	10	10½	11	11½	12
	Number of sts to CO														
5							40							60	60
5½					40							60	60		
6				40						60	60				
6½			40						60						80
7		40						60					80	80	
7½							60					80			
8	40				60						80				
8½			60					80						100	100
9				60					80				100		
9½							80					100			
10			60				80					100			120

TOP-DOWN SOCK

CUFF AND LEG (FOR TOE-UP VERSION, SEE PAGE 45)

Using one of the COs beg on page 73, CO 40 (60, 80, 100, 120) sts. Divide sts per needle as follows:

4 dpn	5 dpn	2 circular needles
(10, 10, 20), (20, 10, 30), (20, 20, 40), (30, 20, 50), (30, 30, 60)	(10, 10, 10, 10), (20, 10, 20, 10), (20, 20, 20, 20), (30, 20, 30, 20), (30, 30, 30, 30)	20 (30, 40, 50, 60)

Join, being careful not to twist sts. Work ribbing for 1½" using suggested ribbing for desired leg pattern (pages 97–100). Work leg to desired length.

HEEL

Work heel on 19 (29, 39, 49, 59) sts, beg with WS row and ending with RS row. Move 1 st from heel to instep as follows to balance patt on instep sts:

Unwork last st on needle 3 and place it on needle 1. Needles 1 and 2: Instep sts Needle 3: Heel sts Sts per needle: (11, 10, 19), (21, 10, 29), (21, 20, 39), (31, 20, 49), (31, 30, 59)	Unwork last st on needle 4 and place it on needle 1. Sl all sts from needle 4 to needle 3. Needles 1 and 2: Instep sts Needle 3: Heel sts Sts per needle: (11, 10, 19), (21, 10, 29), (21, 20, 39), (31, 20, 49), (31, 30, 59)	Unwork last st on needle 2 and place it on needle 1. Needle 1: Instep sts Needle 2: Heel sts Sts per needle: (21, 19), (31, 29), (41, 39), (51, 49), (61, 59)

You have a choice to work "Heel-Flap Heel" (page 44) or "Short-Row Heel" (page 45). If you are working heel-flap heel, cont working until you reach "Short-Row Heel," then skip to "Foot."

HEEL-FLAP HEEL

Work one of heel sts below or refer to "Heel Flaps" (page 66) for other options.

Turn work to beg heel on WS row.

Heel st with chain selvage (sl *last* st, never first st)

Row 1 (WS): K1, purl to last st, sl 1 wyif.

Row 2: K1, *sl 1 wyib, K1, rep from * to last 2 sts, sl 1 wyib, sl 1 wyif.

Note that you will not sl sts at end of rows in foll heel-st patts; you will work a garter-edge selvage for picking up sts along heel flap.

St st with 3-st garter edge

Row 1 (WS): K3, purl to end.

Row 2: P3, knit to end.

Heel st with 3-st garter edge

Row 1 (WS): K3, purl to end.

Row 2: P3, *sl 1, K1, rep from * to last 4 sts, sl 1, K3.

Rep rows 1 and 2 of selected heel-st patt until you have 20 (30, 40, 50, 60) heel-flap rows; last row should be a RS row.

HEEL TURN

Work as follows:

Row 1 (WS): Sl 1, P10 (15, 20, 24, 30), P2tog, P1, turn.

Row 2: Sl 1, K4, ssk, K1, turn. Note that there will be a small gap between working sts that form heel turn and unworked heel sts.

Row 3: Sl 1, purl to within 1 st of gap, P2tog, P1, turn.

Row 4: Sl 1, knit to within 1 st of gap, ssk, K1, turn.

Rep rows 3 and 4, inc 1 additional knit or purl st after the sl 1 until all side sts are worked; end with completed row 4. There should be 11 (17, 21, 27, 31) sts left on heel flap. When working rows 3 and 4, there may be no ending single st to work; some numbers don't work out.

For ease of instructions, beg of rnd is now at center of bottom of foot. The needles are renumbered at this point. Needle 1 is beg of rnd and holds all heel-turn sts.

GUSSET

4 dpn	5 dpn	2 circular needles
Combine instep sts onto needle 2.	Needles 2 and 3: Instep sts	Needle 1: Heel sts Needle 2: Instep sts
With RS facing you and needle 1, PU 10 (15, 20, 25, 30) sts from side of heel flap. PU and knit 2 extra sts at top of gusset (see page 80), then		
Needle 2: Beg where you left off in patt to work heel, work est patt across instep. Needle 3: PU and knit 2 extra sts at top of gusset, PU and knit 10 (15, 20, 25, 30) sts from side of heel flap, K5 (8, 10, 13, 15) from needle 1. Sts per needle: (18, 21, 17), (26, 31, 25), (33, 41, 32), (41, 51, 40), (48, 61, 47)	Needles 2 and 3: Beg where you left off in patt to work heel, work est patt across instep. Needle 4: PU and knit 2 extra sts at top of gusset, PU and knit 10 (15, 20, 25, 30) sts from side of heel flap, K5 (8, 10, 13, 15) from needle 1. Sts per needle: (18, 11, 10, 17), (26, 21, 10, 25), (33, 21, 20, 32), (41, 31, 20, 40), (48, 31, 30, 47)	Cont with needle 1: PM, work 11 (21, 21, 31, 31) sts in patt. Needle 2: Work rem instep sts, PM, PU and knit 2 extra sts at top of gusset, PU and knit 10 (15, 20, 25, 30) sts from side of heel flap, K5 (8, 10, 13, 15) from needle 1. Sts per needle: (29, 27), (47, 35), (54, 52), (72, 60), (79, 77)

CLOSE GUSSET TOP

Needle 1: Knit to last 2 sts, ssk. Needle 2: Work est patt. Needle 3: K2tog, knit to end.	Needle 1: Knit to last 2 sts, ssk. Needles 2 and 3: Work est patt. Needle 4: K2tog, knit to end.	Needle 1: Knit to 2 sts before marker, ssk, SM, work est patt to end. Needle 2: Work est patt to marker, SM, K2tog, knit to end.

GUSSET DECREASE

Rnd 1	**Rnd 1**	**Rnd 1**
Needle 1: Knit to last 3 sts, K2tog, K1. Needle 2: Work est patt. Needle 3: K1, ssk, knit to end.	Needle 1: Knit to last 3 sts, K2tog, K1. Needles 2 and 3: Work est patt. Needle 4: K1, ssk, knit to end.	Needle 1: Knit to 3 sts before marker, K2tog, K1, SM, work est patt. Needle 2: Work est patt to marker, SM, K1, ssk, knit to end.

Rnd 2: Work in est patt on instep sts, and in St st on sole sts.

Rep rnds 1 and 2 until 40 (60, 80, 100, 120) total sts rem. Proceed to "Foot."

SHORT-ROW HEEL

Note that if you work heel sts on 2 needles, unworked sts are not stretched as much as if you use 1 needle. This also lessens the tendency to create gaps at base of heel.

Work heel back and forth on 19 (29, 39, 49, 59) sts, foll instructions for "Short-Row Heel" on page 68. Rep rows 3 and 4 until 7 (11, 15, 19, 23) sts rem unwrapped. End ready for RS row.

Reverse short-row shaping.

With heel-st yarn, knit across heel, knitting wrap with last st of heel. Work across instep; when you get back to heel sts, knit first heel st with wrap.

FOOT

4 dpn	5 dpn	2 circular needles
Cont St st on needles 1 and 3, and est patt on needle 2 to desired heel-to-toe length.	Cont St st on needles 1 and 4, and est patt on needles 2 and 3 to desired heel-to-toe length.	Rearrange sts so instep sts are on needle 1 and sole sts are on needle 2. Markers are no longer needed. Cont est patt to desired heel-to-toe length.

TOE SHAPING

Knit sts on needle 1. Renumber needles: Needle 1: Instep sts Needles 2 and 3: Sole sts Sts per needle: (21, 10, 9), (31, 15, 14), (41, 20, 19), (51, 25, 24), (61, 30, 29)	Knit sts on needle 1. Renumber needles: Needles 1 and 2: Instep sts Needles 3 and 4: Sole sts Sts per needle: (11, 10, 10, 9), (16, 15, 15, 14), (21, 20, 20, 19), (26, 25, 25, 24), (31, 30, 30, 29)	Needle 1: Instep sts Needle 2: Sole sts Sts per needle: (21, 19), (31, 29), (41, 39), (51, 49), (61, 59)

Work toe decs as follows:

Rnd 1	**Rnd 1**	**Rnd 1**
Needle 1: K2, ssk, cont in instep patt to last 4 sts, K2tog, K2. Needle 2: K2, ssk, knit to end. Needle 3: Knit to last 4 sts, K2tog, K2.	Needle 1: K2, ssk, cont in instep patt to end. Needle 2: Cont in instep patt to last 4 sts, K2tog, K2. Needle 3: K2, ssk, knit to end. Needle 4: Knit to last 4 sts, K2tog, K2.	Needle 1: K2, ssk, cont in instep patt to last 4 sts, K2tog, K2. Needle 2: K4, ssk, knit to last 4 sts, K2tog, K2.

Rnd 2: Knit around.

Rep rnds 1 and 2 until 20 (28, 40, 48, 60) total sts rem. Sts for instep and sole are: (11, 9), (15, 13), (21, 19), (25, 23), (31, 29).

Rep rnd 1 only until 10 (14, 18, 26, 30) total sts rem. There are 5 (7, 9, 13, 15) sts each on sole and instep; last 2 dec will be on instep.

Place instep sts on 1 needle and sole sts on 2nd needle. Graft sts tog with kitchener st (page 79).

TOE-UP SOCKS

If you would like to work this sock from the toe up, follow these instructions for toe, and then follow instructions specifically for parts of top-down socks as indicated.

EASY TOE

With waste yarn and provisional CO (see page 76), CO 8 (12, 16, 20, 24) sts. Purl 1 row with sock yarn. Work back and forth in St st for 6 rows or until rectangle is approx ½" high; end on a purl row, call the needle with these sts needle A for 4 dpn and 5 dpn and needle 1 for 2 circulars. Unzip provisional CO sts and place them on spare needle. Beg knitting in rnd.

4 dpn	5 dpn	2 circular needles
With RS facing you, K8 (12, 16, 20, 24) from needle A; cont with needle 1, PU and knit 2 sts from side edge.	With RS facing you, K4 (6, 8, 10, 12) from needle A; these sts will be part of needle 1.	With RS facing you, K8 (12, 16, 20, 24); cont with needle 1, PU and knit 2 sts from side edge.
With needle 2, PU and knit 2 sts from side edge, K4 (6, 8, 10, 12) from spare needle.	With needle 2, K4 (6, 8, 10, 12) from needle A, then PU and knit 2 sts from side edge.	With needle 2, PU and knit 2 sts from side edge, K8, (12, 16, 20, 24) from CO edge, PU and knit 2 sts from side edge.
With needle 3, K4 (6, 8, 10, 12) from spare needle, then PU and knit 2 sts from side edge.	With needle 3, PU and knit 2 sts from side edge, K4 (6, 8, 10, 12) from spare needle.	With needle 1, PU and knit 2 sts from side edge.
With last needle, PU and knit 2 sts from side edge, then knit rem sts from needle 1.	With needle 4, K4 (6, 8, 10, 12) from spare needle, then PU and knit 2 sts from side edge.	Complete rnd by knitting across rem sts on needle 1 and across needle 2.
Complete rnd by knitting across needles 2 and 3.	With needle 5, PU and knit last 2 sts from side edge, K4 (6, 8, 10, 12) from needle 1; this is now needle 1.	Sts per needle: 12 (16, 20, 24, 28)
Sts per needle: (12, 6, 6), (16, 8, 8), (20, 10, 10), (24, 12, 12), (28, 14, 14)	Complete rnd by knitting across needles 2, 3, and 4.	
	Sts per needle: 6 (8, 10, 12, 14)	

Work toe incs as follows:

Rnd 1	**Rnd 1**	**Rnd 1**
Needle 1: K1, M1, knit to last st, M1, K1.	Needle 1: K1, M1, knit to end.	Needle 1: K1, M1, knit to last st, M1, K1.
Needle 2: K1, M1, knit to end.	Needle 2: Knit to last st, M1, K1.	Needle 2: K1, M1, knit to last st, M1, K1.
Needle 3: Knit to last st, M1, K1.	Needle 3: K1, M1, knit to end.	
	Needle 4: Knit to last st, M1, K1.	

Rnd 2: Knit around.

Rep rnds 1 and 2 until 40 (60, 80, 100, 120) total sts rem.

Rearrange sts by moving 1 st from sole to instep. This extra st on instep allows you to balance patt in instep.

Work patt of choice on instep needle(s) until foot is desired length.

Needle 1: Instep sts	Needles 1 and 2: Instep sts	Needle 1: Instep sts
Needles 2 and 3: Sole sts	Needles 3 and 4: Sole sts	Needle 2: Sole sts
Sts per needle: (21, 10, 9), (31, 15, 14), (41, 20, 19), (51, 25, 24), (61, 30, 29)	Sts per needle: (11, 10, 10, 9), (16, 15, 15, 14), (21, 20, 20, 19), (26, 25, 25, 24), (31, 30, 30, 29)	Sts per needle: (21, 19), (31, 29), (41, 39), (51, 49), (61, 59)
Combine sole sts onto needle 3, to become heel sts.	Combine sole sts onto needle 3, to become heel sts.	Sole sts are now heel sts.
Divide instep sts onto needles 1 and 2.		

HEEL

Work "Heel-Flap Heel" (page 44) on heel sts.

When you have completed heel flap and 40 (60, 80, 100, 120) total sts rem, rearrange sts as follows:

(20, 10, 10), (30, 20, 20), (40, 20, 20), (50, 30, 20), (60, 30, 30)	(10, 10, 10, 10), (20, 10, 20, 10), (20, 20, 20, 20), (30, 20, 30, 20), (30, 30, 30, 30)	20 (30, 40, 50, 60)

LEG

Discontinue working extra st on instep patt and cont patt around leg to desired length.

CUFF

Work cuff for 1½" using suggested ribbing for leg patt you worked. BO loosely (page 77).

Twelve-Stitch Patterns

The variety of twelve-stitch patterns is overwhelming. They include a range of lace, knit and purl textures, as well as a knit-and-purl-based pattern. These patterns require an extra stitch for the instep and an odd number of stitches in the heel.

SKILL LEVEL: INTERMEDIATE ◼◼◼▢

Leaf Ribbing sock made with Shepherd Worsted from Lorna's Laces (color 12ns Lilac) on size 4 needles with a gauge of 5½ sts to 1". This sock starts at the top, has a heel with a garter-edged heel flap, and ends with a standard toe.

Stansfield 304 sock made with Lola from Schaefer Yarn (color Blue/Green) on size 3 needles with a gauge of 6¾ sts to 1". The sock starts at the top with a garter-stitch cuff, has a garter-edged heel stitch in the heel, and ends with a standard toe.

Baby Fern sock made with Shepherd Sport from Lorna's Laces (color 50ns Poppy) on size 2 needles with a gauge of 7¼ sts to 1". This sock is knit with a garter-edged stockinette heel and a standard toe.

MATERIALS

Gather materials for the socks you'd like to make and select the pattern you'd like to use.

DIRECTIONS

Select the number of sts to CO based on the gauge for your yarn and needles and the circumference of the intended foot.

SOCK STITCHES

Gauge sts/1"	Foot Circumference in Inches														
	5	5½	6	6½	7	7½	8	8½	9	9½	10	10½	11	11½	12
	Number of sts to CO														
5										48					
5½								48	48						
6							48							72	72
6½						48							72		
7					48						72	72			
7½				48						72					
8			48						72						96
8½		48						72						96	
9							72					96	96		
9½	48					72					96				
10					72					96					120

TOP-DOWN SOCK

CUFF AND LEG (FOR TOE-UP VERSION, SEE PAGE 51)

Using one of the COs beg on page 73, CO 48 (72, 96, 120) sts. Divide sts per needle as follows:

4 dpn	5 dpn	2 circular needles
(12, 12, 24), (24, 12, 36), (24, 24, 48), (36, 24, 60)	(12, 12, 12, 12), (24, 12, 24, 12), (24, 24, 24, 24), (36, 24, 36, 24)	24 (36, 48, 60)

Join, being careful not to twist sts. Work ribbing for 1½" using suggested ribbing for desired leg pattern (pages 100–103). Work leg to desired length.

HEEL

Work heel on 23 (35, 47, 59) sts, beg with WS row and ending with RS row. Move 1 st from heel to instep as follows to balance patt on instep:

Unwork last st on needle 3 and place it on needle 1. Needles 1 and 2: Instep sts Needle 3: Heel sts Sts per needle: (13, 12, 23), (25, 12, 35), (25, 24, 47), (37, 24, 59)	Unwork last st on needle 4 and place it on needle 1. Sl all sts from needle 4 to needle 3. Needles 1 and 2: Instep sts Needle 3: Heel sts Sts per needle: (13, 12, 23), (25, 12, 35), (25, 24, 47), (37, 24, 59)	Unwork last st on needle 2 and place it on needle 1. Needle 1: Instep sts Needle 2: Heel sts Sts per needle: (25, 23), (37, 35), (49, 47), (61, 59)

You have a choice to work "Heel-Flap Heel" (page 49) or "Short-Row Heel" (page 50). If you are working heel-flap heel, cont working until you reach "Short-Row Heel," then skip to "Foot."

HEEL-FLAP HEEL

Work one of heel sts below or refer to "Heel Flaps" (page 66) for other options.

Turn work to beg heel on WS row.

Heel st with 3-st garter edge

Row 1 (WS): K3, purl to end.

Row 2: P3, *K1, sl 1, rep from * to last 4 sts, K4.

St st with 3-st garter edge

Row 1 (WS): K3, purl to end.

Row 2: P3, knit to end.

Rep rows 1 and 2 of selected heel-st patt until you have 24 (36, 48, 60) total rows in heel flap; last row should be a RS row.

HEEL TURN

Work as follows:

Row 1 (WS): Sl 1, P12 (18, 24, 30), P2tog, P1, turn.

Row 2: Sl 1, K4, ssk, K1, turn. Note that there will be a small gap between working sts that form heel turn and unworked heel sts.

Row 3: Sl 1, purl to within 1 st of gap, P2tog, P1, turn.

Row 4: Sl 1, knit to within 1 st of gap, ssk, K1, turn.

Rep rows 3 and 4, inc 1 additional knit or purl st after the sl 1 until all side sts are worked; end with completed row 4. There should be 13 (19, 25, 31) sts left on heel flap.

For ease of instructions, beg of rnd is now at center of bottom of foot. The needles are renumbered at this point. Needle 1 is beg of rnd and holds all heel-turn sts.

GUSSET

4 dpn	5 dpn	2 circular needles
Combine instep sts onto needle 2.	Needles 2 and 3: Instep sts	Needle 1: Heel sts Needle 2: Instep sts

With RS facing you and needle 1, PU and knit 12 (18, 24, 30) sts from side of heel flap, PU and knit 2 sts at top of gusset (see page 80), then

Needle 2: Work across instep in est patt. Needle 3: PU and knit 2 sts at top of gusset, PU and knit 12 (18, 24, 30) sts from side of heel flap, K6 (9, 12, 15) from needle 1. Sts per needle: (21, 25, 20), (30, 37, 29), (39, 49, 38), (48, 61, 47)	Needles 2 and 3: Work across instep in est patt. Needle 4: PU and knit 2 sts at top of gusset, PU and knit 12 (18, 24, 30) sts from side of heel flap, K6 (9, 12, 15) from needle 1. Sts per needle: (21, 13, 12, 20), (30, 25, 12, 29), (39, 25, 24, 38), (48, 37, 24, 47)	PM, work 13 (25, 25, 37) instep sts in est patt. Needle 2: Work rem instep sts in est patt, PM, PU and knit 2 sts at top of gusset, PU and knit 12 (18, 24, 30) sts from side of heel flap, K6 (9, 12, 15) from needle 1. The needles now hold left half and right half of sock. Sts per needle: (34, 32), (55, 41), (64, 62), (85, 71)

CLOSE GUSSET TOP

Needle 1: Knit to last 2 sts, ssk. Needle 2: Work est patt. Needle 3: K2tog, knit to end.	Needle 1: Knit to last 2 sts, ssk. Needles 2 and 3: Work est patt. Needle 4: K2tog, knit to end.	Needle 1: Knit to 2 sts before marker, ssk, SM, work est patt to end. Needle 2: Work est patt to marker, SM, K2tog, knit to end.

GUSSET DECREASE

Rnd 1	**Rnd 1**	**Rnd 1**
Needle 1: Knit to last 3 sts, K2tog, K1. Needle 2: Work est patt. Needle 3: K1, ssk, knit to end.	Needle 1: Knit to last 3 sts, K2tog, K1. Needles 2 and 3: Work est patt. Needle 4: K1, ssk, knit to end.	Needle 1: Knit to 3 sts before marker, K2tog, K1, SM, work est patt. Needle 2: Work est patt to marker, SM, K1, ssk, knit to end.

Rnd 2: Work in est patt on instep sts, and in St st on sole sts.

Rep rnds 1 and 2 until 48 (72, 96, 120) total sts rem. Proceed to "Foot."

SHORT-ROW HEEL

Note that if you work heel sts on 2 needles, unworked sts are not stretched as much as if you use 1 needle. This also lessens the tendency to create gaps at base of heel.

Work heel on 23 (35, 47, 59) sts, foll instructions for "Short-Row Heel" on page 68. Rep rows 3 and 4 until 9 (13, 19, 23) sts rem unwrapped. End ready for a RS row.

Reverse short-row shaping.

With heel-st yarn, knit across heel, knitting wrap with last st of heel. Work across instep; when you get back to heel sts, knit first heel st with wrap.

FOOT

4 dpn	5 dpn	2 circular needles
Cont St st on needles 1 and 3, and est patt on needle 2 to desired heel-to-toe length.	Cont St st on needles 1 and 4, and est patt on needles 2 and 3 to desired heel-to-toe length.	Rearrange sts so instep sts are on needle 1 and sole sts are on needle 2. Markers are no longer needed. Cont est patt to desired heel-to-toe length.

TOE SHAPING

Typically, toes are knit in St st, but you have a choice to cont patt from instep through whole toe; either pay attention and work as it flows, or draw patt on graph paper to keep track of where you are.

Adjust beg of rnd to side of foot as follows:

Knit sts on needle 1. Renumber needles. Needle 1: Instep sts Needles 2 and 3: Sole sts Sts per needle: (25, 11, 12), (37, 17, 18), (49, 23, 24), (61, 29, 30)	Knit sts on needle 1. Renumber needles. Needles 1 and 2: Instep sts Needles 3 and 4: Sole sts Sts per needle: (12, 13, 11, 12), (18, 19, 17, 18), (24, 25, 23, 24), (30, 31, 29, 30)	Needle 1: Instep sts Needle 2: Sole sts Sts per needle: (25, 23), (37, 35), (49, 47), (61, 59)

Work toe decs as follows:

Rnd 1	**Rnd 1**	**Rnd 1**
Needle 1: K1, ssk, cont in instep patt to last 3 sts, K2tog, K1. Needle 2: K1, ssk, knit to end. Needle 3: Knit to last 3 sts, K2tog, K1.	Needle 1: K1, ssk, cont in instep patt to end. Needle 2: Cont in instep patt to last 3 sts, K2tog, K1. Needle 3: K1, ssk, knit to end. Needle 4: Knit to last 3 sts, K2tog, K1.	Needle 1: K1, ssk, cont in instep patt to last 3 sts, K2tog, K1. Needle 2: K1, ssk, knit to last 3 sts, K2tog, K1.

Rnd 2: Knit around.

Rep rnds 1 and 2 until 24 (36, 48, 60) total sts rem. Sts for instep and sole are: (13, 11), (19, 17), (25, 23), (31, 29).

Rep rnd 1 only until 14 (22, 26, 34) total sts rem. There are 7 (11, 13, 17) sts each on sole and instep; last 2 dec will be on instep.

Place instep sts on 1 needle and sole sts on 2nd needle. Graft sts tog with kitchener st (page 79).

TOE-UP INSTRUCTIONS

If you would like to work this sock from the toe up, follow these instructions for toe, and then follow instructions specifically for parts of top-down sock as indicated.

EASY TOE

With waste yarn and provisional CO (see page 76), CO 10 (14, 20, 24) sts. Purl 1 row with sock yarn. Work back and forth in St st for 6 rows or until rectangle is approx ½" high; end on a purl row, call the needle with these sts needle A for 4 dpn and 5 dpn and needle 1 for 2 circulars. Unzip provisional CO sts and place them on spare needle. Beg knitting in rnd.

4 dpn	5 dpn	2 circular needles
With RS facing you, K10 (14, 20, 24) from needle A; cont with needle 1, PU and knit 2 sts from side edge. With needle 2, PU and knit 2 sts from side edge, K5 (7, 10, 12) from spare needle. With needle 3, K5 (7, 10, 12) from spare needle, then PU and knit 2 sts from side edge. With last needle, PU and knit 2 sts from side edge, then knit rem sts from needle 1. Complete rnd by knitting across needles 2 and 3. Sts per needle: (14, 7, 7), (18, 9, 9), (24, 12, 12), (28, 14, 14)	With RS facing you, K5 (7, 10, 12) from needle A; these sts will be part of needle 1. With needle 2, K5 (7, 10, 12) from needle A, then PU and knit 2 sts from side edge. With needle 3, PU and knit 2 more sts from side edge, K5 (7, 10, 12) from spare needle. With needle 4, K5 (7, 10, 12) from spare needle, then PU and knit 2 sts from side edge. With needle 5, PU and knit last 2 sts from side edge, K5 (7, 10, 12) sts from needle 1; this is needle 1. Complete rnd by knitting across needles 2, 3, and 4. Sts per needle: 7 (9, 12, 14)	With RS facing you, K10 (14, 20, 24); cont with needle 1, PU and knit 2 sts from side edge. With needle 2, PU and knit 2 sts from side edge, K10 (14, 20, 24) from CO edge, PU and knit 2 sts from side edge. With needle 1, PU and knit 2 sts from side edge. Complete rnd by knitting across rem sts on needle 1 and across needle 2. Sts per needle: 14 (18, 24, 28)

Work toe incs as follows:

Rnd 1	**Rnd 1**	**Rnd 1**
Needle 1: K1, M1, knit to last st, M1, K1. Needle 2: K1, M1, knit to end. Needle 3: Knit to last st, M1, K1.	Needle 1: K1, M1, knit to end. Needle 2: Knit to last st, M1, K1. Needle 3: K1, M1, knit to end. Needle 4: Knit to last st, M1, K1.	Needle 1: K1, M1, knit to last st, M1, K1. Needle 2: K1, M1, knit to last st, M1, K1.

Rnd 2: Knit around.

Rep rnds 1 and 2 until 48 (72, 96, 120) total sts rem.

Rearrange sts by moving 1 st from sole to instep. This extra st on instep allows you to balance patt in instep.

Work patt of choice on instep needle(s) until foot is desired length.

| Needle 1: Instep sts
Needles 2 and 3: Sole sts
Sts per needle: (25, 11, 12), (37, 17, 18), (49, 23, 24), (61, 29, 30)
Combine sole sts onto needle 3, to become heel sts.
Divide instep sts onto needles 1 and 2. | Needles 1 and 2: Instep sts
Needles 3 and 4: Sole sts
Sts per needle: (12, 13, 11, 12), (18, 19, 17, 18), (24, 25, 23, 24), (30, 31, 29, 30)
Combine sole sts onto needle 3, to become heel sts. | Needle 1: Instep sts
Needle 2: Sole sts
Sts per needle: (25, 23), (37, 35), (49, 47), (61, 59)
Sole sts are now heel sts. |

HEEL

Work "Heel-Flap Heel" (page 49) or "Short-Row Heel" (page 50) on heel sts.

When you have completed heel and gusset or short-row heel and 48 (72, 96, 120) sts rem, rearrange sts as follows:

(12, 12, 24), (18, 18, 36), (24, 24, 48), (30, 30, 60)	12 (18, 24, 30)	24 (36, 48, 60)

LEG

Discontinue working extra st on instep patt and cont patt around leg to desired length.

CUFF

Work cuff for 1½" using suggested ribbing for leg patt you worked. BO loosely (page 77).

Six-Stitch Stranded Patterns

Socks made with stranded patterns are less elastic than socks knit with only one yarn. These patterns have related leg and foot patterns. The foot pattern is a small portion of the larger pattern, creating a different pattern yet harmonious whole for the sock. Additionally, all the patterns selected have a round of one-color knitting in the sequence. This is great news for knitting a sock with a heel flap. If you begin the heel in the round before the solid one, you can then begin picking up stitches for the heel flap and gusset with only one yarn to work. All of the instep patterns are subsets of the leg pattern.

SKILL LEVEL: EXPERIENCED ◀■■■

Arches sock made with Jawoll Superwash from Lang Yarns (colors 61 Red and 59 Orange) on size 1 needles with a gauge of 9½ sts to 1". This sock has a heel with a garter-edged, pinstriped heel stitch and a pinstriped star toe.

Hourglass sock made with Meilenweit 6 fach from Lana Grossa (colors 30 Green and 35 Yellow) on size 1 needles with a gauge of 8¼ sts to 1". This sock has a heel with a solid, garter-edged heel stitch and a solid star toe.

Diamonds sock made with Gems Merino Opal from Louet Sales (colors 51 Pink Panther and 42 Eggplant) on size 2 needles with a gauge of 8½ sts to 1". This sock has a heel with a solid, garter-edged heel stitch and a pinstriped star toe.

MATERIALS

Gather materials for the socks you'd like to make and select the pattern you'd like to use.

DIRECTIONS

Select the number of sts to CO based on the gauge for your yarn and needles and the circumference of the intended foot.

SOCK STITCHES

Gauge sts/1"	Foot Circumference in Inches														
	5	5½	6	6½	7	7½	8	8½	9	9½	10	10½	11	11½	12
	Number of sts to CO														
5					36					48				60	60
5½				36				48	48			60	60		
6			36				48				60				72
6½		36				48				60			72	72	
7	36				48			60			72	72			84
7½				48			60			72			84	84	
8			48			60			72			84			96
8½		48			60			72			84		96	96	
9				60			72			84		96			108
9½	48					72			84		96			108	
10			60		72			84		96			108		120

CUFF AND LEG

Using one of the COs beg on page 73 and dark yarn, CO 36 (48, 60, 72, 84, 96, 108, 120) sts. Divide sts per needle as follows:

4 dpn	5 dpn	2 circular needles
(6, 12, 18), (12, 12, 24), (12, 18, 30), (18, 18, 36), (18, 24, 42), (24, 24, 48), (24, 30, 54), (30, 30, 60)	(6, 12, 6, 12), (12, 12, 12, 12), (12, 18, 12, 18), (18, 18, 18, 18), (18, 24, 18, 24), (24, 24, 24, 24), (24, 30, 24, 30), (30, 30, 30, 30)	18 (24, 30, 36, 42, 48, 54, 60)

Join, being careful not to twist sts, and work K2, P2 ribbing or ribbing of choice for 1½". Beg leg patt of choice (pages 103–105) and work to desired leg length. Arches sock is knit with 3 reps of chart, then rnds 1 and 2.

HEEL FLAP

Work heel on 17 (23, 29, 35, 41, 47, 53, 59) sts, starting with WS row and ending with RS row. Move 1 st from heel to instep as follows to balance patt on instep:

Unwork last st on needle 3 and place it on needle 1. Needles 1 and 2: Instep sts Needle 3: Heel sts Sts per needle: (7, 12, 17), (13, 12, 23), (13, 18, 29), (19, 18, 35), (19, 24, 41), (25, 24, 47), (25, 30, 53), (31, 30, 59)	Unwork last st on needle 4 and place it on needle 1. Sl all sts from needle 4 to needle 3. Needles 1 and 2: Instep sts Needle 3: Heel sts Sts per needle: (7, 12, 17), (13, 12, 23), (13, 18, 29), (19, 18, 35), (19, 24, 41), (25, 24, 47), (25, 30, 53), (31, 30, 59)	Unwork last st on needle 2 and place it on needle 1. Needle 1: Instep sts Needle 2: Heel sts Sts per needle: (19, 17), (25, 23), (31, 29), (37, 35), (43, 41), (49, 47), (55, 53), (61, 59)

Work one of heel-st patts below or refer to "Heel Flaps" (page 66) for other options.

Turn work to beg heel on WS row.

Heel st in 2 colors with 3-st garter edge

Work rows 1 and 2 with dark only.

Row 1 (WS): K3, purl to end of needle.

Row 2: P3, *K1, sl 1, rep from * to last 4 sts, K4.

Work rows 3 and 4 with dark and light.

Row 3: K3 with dark, *P1 with light, P1 with dark, rep to last 4 sts, P1 with light, P3 with dark.

Row 4: P3 with dark, *sl 1, K1, rep from *, weaving in slipped color across to last 4 sts, K4.

Rep rows 3 and 4 to desired heel height; end by working RS row.

Heel st in solid color with 3-st garter edge

Row 1 (WS): K3, purl to end.

Row 2: P3, *sl 1, K1, rep from * to last 4 sts, sl 1, K3.

Rep rows 1 and 2 until you have 18 (24, 30, 36, 42, 48, 54, 60) heel-flap rows; last row should be a RS row.

HEEL TURN

Work in dark only.

Row 1 (WS): Sl 1, P9 (12, 15, 18, 21, 24, 27, 30), P2tog, P1, turn.

Row 2: Sl 1, K4, ssk, K1, turn. Note that there will be a small gap between working sts that form heel turn and unworked heel sts.

Row 3: Sl 1, purl to within 1 st of gap, P2tog (1 st on either side of gap), P1, turn.

Row 4: Sl 1, knit to within 1 st of gap, ssk, K1, turn.

Rep rows 3 and 4, inc 1 additional knit or purl st after sl 1 until all side sts are worked, ending with RS row. There are 11 (13, 17, 19, 23, 25, 29, 31) sts rem on heel flap.

For ease of instructions, beg of rnd is now at center of bottom of foot. The needles have been renumbered at this point. Needle 1 is beg of rnd and holds all heel sts.

GUSSET

Rearrange sts and renumber needles as follows:

4 dpn	5 dpn	2 circular needles
Combine instep sts onto needle 2.	Needles 2 and 3: Instep sts	Needle 1: Heel sts Needle 2: Instep sts

With RS facing you, needle 1, and dark, PU and knit 1 st for each garter bump and 2 extra sts at top of gusset (see page 80), then

Needle 2: With dark, work across. Needle 3: With dark, PU and knit 2 extra sts at top of gusset, then PU and knit 1 st for each garter bump, K5 (6, 8, 9, 11, 12, 14, 15) from needle 1.	Needles 2 and 3: With dark, work across. Needle 4: With dark, PU and knit 2 extra sts at top of gusset, then PU and knit 1 st for each garter bump, K5 (6, 8, 9, 11, 12, 14, 15) from needle 1.	Cont with needle 1 and dark, PM, work (13, 13, 19, 19, 25, 25, 31, 31) sts. Needle 2: With dark, work rem sts, PM, PU and knit 2 extra sts at top of gusset, then PU and knit 1 st for each garter bump, K5 (6, 8, 9, 11, 12, 14, 15) from needle 1.

Sole of sock is worked in same foot patt as instep. Gusset dec is worked in pinstripe patt. With center of heel facing you, count and PM after 8 (11, 14, 17, 20, 23, 26, 29) sts from center back of sole on needle 1, and

on needle 3, PM at 9 (12, 15, 18, 21, 24, 27, 30) sts from bottom center of foot. Sts per needle: (17, 19, 16), (21, 25, 20), (26, 31, 25), (30, 37, 29), (35, 43, 34), (39, 49, 38), (44, 55, 43), (48, 61, 47)	on needle 4, PM at 9 (12, 15, 18, 21, 24, 27, 30) sts from bottom center of foot. Sts per needle: (17, 7, 12, 16), (21, 13, 12, 20), (26, 13, 18, 25), (30, 19, 18, 29), (35, 19, 24, 34), (39, 25, 24, 38), (44, 25, 30, 43), (48, 31, 30, 47)	on needle 2, PM at 9 (12, 15, 18, 21, 24, 27, 30) sts from bottom center of foot. Sts per needle: (30, 22), (34, 32), (45, 37), (49, 47), (60, 52), (64, 62), (75, 67), (79, 77). Needles now hold left and right sides of sock.

CLOSE GUSSET TOP

The contrast or light is waiting at top of gusset.

Needle 1: With dark, knit to last 2 sts, ssk, SM when necessary. Needle 2: Beg rnd 1 of foot chart with dark and light. Needle 3: Work pinstripe patt as follows: K2tog with dark, *K1 with light, K1 with dark, rep from * to marker, cont foot patt from needle 1.	Needle 1: With dark, knit to last 2 sts, ssk, SM when necessary. Needles 2 and 3: Beg rnd 1 of foot chart with dark and light. Needle 4: Work pinstripe patt as follows: K2tog with dark, *K1 with light, K1 with dark, rep from * to marker, cont foot patt from needle 1.	Needle 1: Knit with dark to 2 sts before 2nd marker (just before instep), ssk, SM, beg rnd 1 of foot chart with dark and light. Needle 2: Cont pinstripe patt to first marker, SM, work pinstripe patt as follows: K2tog with dark, *K1 with light, K1 with dark, rep from * to marker, cont foot patt from instep.

GUSSET DECREASE

Pay attention to where on chart you are for foot; you may need to move 1 or 2 sts to have needle 1 beg with first st of patt rep. It makes it easier to keep track of where you are.

There are 2 beg of rnd at this point: the dec beg with needle 1 and patt beg on instep.

4 dpn	5 dpn	2 circular needles
Rnd 1 Needle 1: Work foot patt to marker, SM, work pinstripe patt. Needle 2: Work foot patt. Needle 3: Work pinstripe patt to marker, SM, work foot patt. **Rnd 2** Needle 1: Work foot patt to marker, SM, work pinstripe patt as follows: knit each dark st with dark and each light st with light to last 3 sts, K2tog with light, K1 with dark. Needle 2: Work foot patt. Needle 3: K1 with dark, ssk with light, work pinstripe patt to marker, SM, cont est foot patt.	**Rnd 1** Needle 1: Work foot patt to marker, SM, work pinstripe patt. Needles 2 and 3: Work foot patt. Needle 4: Work pinstripe patt to marker, SM, work foot patt. **Rnd 2** Needle 1: Work foot patt to marker, SM, work pinstripe patt as follows: knit each dark st with dark and each light st with light to last 3 sts, K2tog with light, K1 with dark. Needles 2 and 3: Work foot patt. Needle 4: K1 with dark, ssk with light, work pinstripe patt to marker, SM, cont est foot patt.	**Rnd 1** Needle 1: Work foot patt to marker, SM, work pinstripe patt to 2nd marker, SM, work foot patt. Needle 2: Work est patt to marker, SM, work pinstripe patt to marker, SM, work foot patt. **Rnd 2** Needle 1: Work foot patt to first marker, SM, work pinstripe patt as follows: knit each dark st with dark and each light st with light to last 3 sts before 2nd marker, K2tog with light, K1 with dark, SM, work est patt. Needle 2: Work est patt to first marker, SM, K1 with dark, ssk with light, work pinstripe patt to 2nd marker, SM, cont est foot patt.

Rep rnds 1 and 2 until 36 (48, 60, 72, 84, 96, 108, 120) total sts rem.

| N/A | N/A | Rearrange sts so instep sts are on needle 1 and sole sts are on needle 2. Markers are no longer needed. |

FOOT

Cont working foot patt to desired heel-to-toe length.

TOE SHAPING

Knit sts on needle 1. Beg of rnd now shifts to side of foot ready to work instep.	Knit sts on needle 1. Beg of rnd now shifts to side of foot ready to work instep.	N/A

Starting at side of foot, beg rnd 1 of patt from chart.
Arrange sts per needle as follows:

(9, 9, 18), (12, 12, 24), (15, 15, 30), (18, 18, 36), (21, 21, 42), (24, 24, 48), (27, 27, 54), (30, 30, 60)	9 (12, 15, 18, 21, 24, 27, 30)	18 (24, 30, 36, 42, 48, 54, 60)

Work toe pinstripe patt as follows: K1 with dark, K1 with light. This will place you at end of each needle with 2 sts to work in dark.

STAR TOE

The foll instructions are for a pinstriped toe. If you want to work toe in solid color, follow instructions below for shaping only. Beg with needle 1.

Rnd 1	**Rnd 1**	**Rnd 1**
Needle 1: Work in pinstripe for 7 (10, 13, 16, 19, 22, 25, 28) sts, K2tog in dark. Needle 2: Work in pinstripe for 7 (10, 13, 16, 19, 22, 25, 28) sts, K2tog in dark. Needle 3: Work in pinstripe for 7 (10, 13, 16, 19, 22, 25, 28) sts, K2tog in dark. PM, work in pinstripe for 7 (10, 13, 16, 19, 22, 25, 28) sts, K2tog in dark.	Work to 2 sts before end of each needle, K2tog. Rep around. (There will be 1 less st between K2tog in next rnd-1 rep.)	Needle 1: Work in pinstripe for 7 (10, 13, 16, 19, 22, 25, 28) sts, K2tog in dark, PM, work in pinstripe for 7 (10, 13, 16, 19, 22, 25, 28) sts, K2tog in dark. Needle 2: Work in pinstripe for 7 (10, 13, 16, 19, 22, 25, 28) sts, K2tog in dark, PM, work in pinstripe for 7 (10, 13, 16, 19, 22, 25, 28) sts, K2tog in dark.

Rnd 2: Knit in pinstripe patt around.

Rnd 3: Work in pinstripe to 2 sts before marker or end of needle, K2tog. Rep around; there will be 1 less st between K2tog in next rnd-3 rep.

Work rnds 2 and 3 another 6 times.

Next rnd: Rep rnd 1 until 8 total sts rem.

Cut yarn, leaving 12" tail. Thread tail onto darning needle and pull through rem sts firmly.

SIX-STITCH TESSELLATED PATTERNS

Tessellated patterns repeat a single shape in two or more colors. A checkerboard is a simple tessellated pattern; if worked in black and white, it is the pattern we all know. However, if it is worked in three colors, the pattern becomes more complex. Many fiber mediums use this style of patterning, including knitting, quilting, and traditional felt work. As you can see from the samples, some are done in multiple colors and one is done in two colors; all are visually interesting and fun to knit. This pattern also offers you a variety of ways to decorate the foot, with a series of instep and sole patterns to make these truly distinctive socks.

SKILL LEVEL: EXPERIENCED ■■■■

Faux Entrelac sock made with Gems Merino Opal from Louet Sales (colors 53 Caribou, 02 Tobacco, 55 Willow, 50 Sage, 47 Terra Cotta, and 62 Citrus Orange) on size 2 needles at a gauge of 7½ sts to 1". This easy-to-work alternative to real entrelac has a garter-edged, stockinette-stitch heel with stars on the instep; pinstriping on the sole; and a solid, standard toe.

Waves sock made with Shepherd Sport from Lorna's Laces (colors 7ns Cedar, 49ns Periwinkle, 45ns Cranberry, and 41ns China Blue) on size 2 needles with a gauge of 8½ sts to 1". This sock starts at the top; has a garter-edged, eye-of-partridge heel; and ends with a solid, standard toe.

Heart Crook sock made with Shepherd Sport from Lorna's Laces (colors 10ns Peach and 22ns Turquoise) on size 2 needles with a gauge of 9 sts to 1". This interesting sock is made with corrugated K1, P1 ribbing and a two-color tessellated pattern with the heel in chain, selvage-edged, pinstriped heel stitch. The sole is worked with pinstriping and a shaped instep. The toe continues in pinstriping and finishes with a mitten-type toe.

Komi Vine sock made with Sock! from Lisa Souza (colors Bronze, Garnet, Yellow Ribbon, Denim, and Turqua) on size 1 needles with a gauge of 11 sts to 1". This sock is made with a garter-edged, eye-of-partridge heel and only two colors on the foot. It uses a cellular pattern on the instep, the traditional Scandinavian lice pattern on the heel, and ends with a six-gore toe.

MATERIALS

Gather materials for the socks you'd like to make and select the pattern you'd like to use.

DIRECTIONS

Select the number of sts to CO based on the gauge for your yarn and needles and the circumference of the intended foot.

SOCK STITCHES

Gauge sts/1"	Foot Circumference in Inches														
	5	5½	6	6½	7	7½	8	8½	9	9½	10	10½	11	11½	12
	Number of sts to CO														
5					36					48				60	60
5½				36				48	48			60	60		
6			36				48					60			72
6½		36				48			60	60			72	72	
7	36				48			60			72	72			84
7½			48				60				72		84	84	
8			48			60			72			84			96
8½		48			60			72			84		96	96	
9			60			72			84			96			108
9½	48					72			84		96			108	
10			60		72			84		96			108		120

CUFF AND LEG

Using one of the COs beg on page 73 and MC, CO 36 (48, 60, 72, 84, 96, 108, 120) sts. Divide sts per needle as follows:

4 dpn	5 dpn	2 circular needles
(6, 12, 18), (12, 12, 24), (12, 18, 30), (18, 18, 36), (18, 24, 42), (24, 24, 48), (24, 30, 54), (30, 30, 60)	(6, 12, 6, 12), (12, 12, 12, 12), (12, 18, 12, 18), (18, 18, 18, 18), (18, 24, 18, 24), (24, 24, 24, 24), (24, 30, 24, 30), (30, 30, 30, 30)	18 (24, 30, 36, 42, 48, 54, 60)

Join, being careful not to twist sts, and work K2, P2 ribbing or ribbing of choice for 1½". Beg leg patt of choice (pages 105–107) and work to desired leg length.

HEEL FLAP

Work heel on 17 (23, 29, 35, 41, 47, 53, 59) sts, beg with WS row and ending with RS row. Move 1 st from heel to instep as follows to balance patt on instep:

Unwork last st on needle 3 and place it on needle 1. Needles 1 and 2: Instep sts Needle 3: Heel sts Sts per needle (7, 12, 17), (13, 12, 23), (13, 18, 29), (19, 18, 35), (19, 24, 41), (25, 24, 47), (25, 30, 53), (31, 30, 59)	Unwork last st on needle 4 and place it on needle 1. Sl all sts from needle 4 to needle 3. Needles 1 and 2: Instep sts Needle 3: Heel sts. Sts per needle (7, 12, 17), (13, 12, 23), (13, 18, 29), (19, 18, 35), (19, 24, 41), (25, 24, 47), (25, 30, 53), (31, 30, 59)	Unwork last st on needle 2 and place it on needle 1. Needle 1: Instep sts Needle 2: Heel sts Sts per needle: (19, 17), (25, 23), (31, 29), (37, 35), (43, 41), (49, 47), (55, 53), (61, 59)

Work one of heel-st patts below or refer to "Heel Flaps" (page 66) for other options.

Turn work to beg heel on WS row.

Heel patt for faux entrelac sock with 3-st garter edge

Row 1 (WS): With MC, K3, purl to end.

Row 2: P3, knit to end of row.

Rep rows 1 and 2 until you've worked 18 (24, 30, 36, 42, 48, 54, 60) heel-flap rows; last row should be a RS row.

Heel patt with eye-of-partridge heel and 3-st garter edge

Rows 1 and 3 (WS): With MC, K3, purl to end.

Row 2: P3, *sl 1, K1, rep from * to last 4 sts, sl 1, K3.

Row 4: P3, *K1, sl 1, rep from * to last 4 sts, K4.

Rep rows 1–4 until you've worked 18 (24, 30, 36, 42, 48, 54, 60) heel-flap rows; last row should be a RS row.

HEEL TURN

Work in MC only.

Row 1 (WS): Sl 1, P9 (12, 15, 18, 21, 24, 27, 30), P2tog, P1, turn.

Row 2: Sl 1, K4, ssk, K1, turn. Note that there will be a small gap between working sts that form heel turn and unworked heel sts.

Row 3: Sl 1, purl to within 1 st of gap, P2tog (1 st on either side of gap), P1, turn.

Row 4: Sl 1, knit to within 1 st of gap, ssk, K1, turn.

Rep rows 3 and 4, inc 1 additional knit or purl st after sl 1 until all side sts are worked, ending with RS row. There are 11 (13, 17, 19, 23, 25, 29, 31) sts rem on heel flap.

Beg of rnd is now at center of bottom of foot. The needles are renumbered at this point. Needle 1 is beg of rnd and holds all heel-turn sts.

GUSSET

Rearrange sts and renumber needles as follows:

4 dpn	5 dpn	2 circular needles
Combine instep sts onto needle 2.	Needles 2 and 3: Instep sts	Needle 1: Heel sts Needle 2: Instep sts

With RS facing you, needle 1, and MC, PU and knit 9 (12, 15, 18, 21, 24, 27, 30) sts and 2 extra sts at top of gusset (see page 80), then

Needle 2: With MC, work across instep. Needle 3: PU and knit 2 extra sts at top of gusset, then PU and knit 1 st for each garter bump, K5 (6, 8, 9, 11, 12, 14, 15) from needle 1. Sts per needle: (17, 19, 16), (21, 25, 20), (26, 31, 25), (30, 37, 29), (35, 43, 34), (39, 49, 38), (44, 55, 43), (48, 61, 47)	Needles 2 and 3: With MC, work across instep. Needle 4: PU and knit 2 extra sts at top of gusset, then PU and knit 1 st for each garter bump, K5 (6, 8, 9, 11, 12, 14, 15) from needle 1. Sts per needle: (17, 7, 12, 16), (21, 13, 12, 20), (26, 13, 18, 25), (30, 19, 18, 29), (35, 19, 24, 34), (39, 25, 24, 38), (44, 25, 30, 43), (48, 31, 30, 47)	Cont with needle 1, PM, work 13 (13, 19, 19, 25, 25, 31, 31) sts with MC. Needle 2: Work rem sts, PM, PU and knit 2 extra sts at top of gusset, then PU and knit 1 st for each garter bump, K5 (6, 8, 9, 11, 12, 14, 15) from needle 1. Sts per needle: (30, 22), (34, 32), (45, 37), (49, 47), (60, 52), (64, 62), (75, 67), (79, 77)

CLOSE GUSSET TOP

Needle 1: With MC, knit to last 2 sts, ssk. Needle 2: Beg rnd 1 of foot chart with MC and CC. Needle 3: Work pinstripe patt as follows: K2tog with MC, *K1 with CC, K1 with MC, rep from * to end.	Needle 1: With MC, knit to last 2 sts, ssk. Needles 2 and 3: Beg rnd 1 of foot chart with MC and CC. Needle 4: Work pinstripe patt as follows: K2tog with MC, *K1 with CC, K1 with MC, rep from * to end.	Needle 1: With MC, knit to 2 sts before marker (just before instep), ssk, SM, beg rnd 1 of foot chart with MC and CC. Needle 2: Cont foot patt to marker, SM, work pinstripe patt as follows: K2tog with MC, *K1 with CC, K1 with MC, rep from * to end.

There are 2 beg of rnd at this point: dec beg with needle 1 and patt beg on instep.

GUSSET DECREASE

Rnd 1 Needle 1: Cont pinstripe patt from previous rnd to last 3 sts, K2tog with CC, K1 with MC. Needle 2: Work est patt. Needle 3: K1 with MC, ssk with CC, work pinstripe patt as est.	**Rnd 1** Needle 1: Cont pinstripe patt from previous rnd to last 3 sts, K2tog with CC, K1 with MC. Needles 2 and 3: Work est patt. Needle 4: K1 with MC, ssk with CC, work pinstripe patt as est.	**Rnd 1** Needle 1: Cont pinstripe patt to last 3 sts before marker, K2tog with CC, K1 with MC, SM, work est patt. Needle 2: Work est patt to first marker, SM, K1 with MC, ssk with CC, work pinstripe patt as est.
Rnd 2 Needle 1: Work pinstripe patt. Needle 2: Work est patt. Needle 3: Work pinstripe patt.	**Rnd 2** Needle 1: Work pinstripe patt. Needles 2 and 3: Work est patt. Needle 4: Work pinstripe patt.	**Rnd 2** Needle 1: Cont pinstripe patt to marker, SM, work est patt. Needle 2: Work est patt, SM, work pinstripe patt. Rearrange sts so instep sts are on needle 1 and sole sts are on needle 2. Markers are no longer needed.

Rep rnds 1 and 2 until 36 (48, 60, 72, 84, 96, 108, 120) total sts rem. Sts for instep and sole are: (19, 17), (25, 23), (31, 29), (37, 35), (43, 41), (49, 47), (55, 53), (61, 59).

At same time, PM before center st on sole, just after 8 (11, 14, 17, 20, 23, 26, 29) sts of sole. Cont working sole in est pinstripe patt, but work "EZ-Shaped Instep" below.

EZ-SHAPED INSTEP (Inspired by Elizabeth Zimmerman, *Wool Gathering* No. 55, Sept '96, Schoolhouse Press)

Work shaped arch on sole sts:

Rnd 1: Knit to 4 sts before marker, K2tog, K2, SM, M1, K1, M1, K2, ssk, knit rem sole sts, work in patt around.

Rnd 2: Work in patt around.

Rnd 3: Knit to 5 sts before marker, K2tog, K3, SM, M1, K1, M1, K3, ssk, knit rem sole sts, work in patt around.

Rnd 4: Work in patt around.

Rnd 5: Knit to 6 sts before marker, K2tog, K4, SM, M1, K1, M1, K4, ssk, knit rem sole sts, work in patt around.

Rnd 6: Work in patt around.

Rnd 7: Knit to 7 st before marker, K2tog, K5, SM, M1, K1, M1, K5, ssk, knit rem sole sts, work in patt around.

Rnd 8: Work in patt around.

Rnd 9: Knit to 8 sts before marker, K2tog, K6, SM, M1, K1, M1, K6, ssk, knit rem sole st, work in patt around.

Rnd 10: Work in patt around.

Cont in est patt, beg K2tog 1 st earlier on each odd round and knitting the ssk 1 st later. Discontinue arch shaping when all heel sts have been included in arch shaping or you are ready to shape toe. Be sure to watch how patt places 3 of same color at center of foot after 1 inc and 2 of same color at dec line, working out on side; next patt round will take you back to pinstripe patt. You may not want to work last patt round to maintain pinstripe on sole.

STANDARD TOE

Toe is worked with MC only.

4 dpn	5 dpn	2 circular needles
Knit sts on needle 1. Renumber needles. Needle 1: Instep sts Needles 2 and 3: Sole sts Sts per needle: (19, 9, 8), (25, 12, 11), (31, 15, 14), (37, 18, 17), (43, 21, 20), (49, 24, 23), (55, 27, 26), (61, 30, 29)	Knit sts on needle 1. Renumber needles. Needles 1 and 2: Instep sts Needles 3 and 4: Sole sts Sts per needle: (10, 9, 9, 8), (13, 12, 12, 11), (16, 15, 15, 14), (19, 18, 18, 17), (22, 21, 21, 20), (25, 24, 24, 23), (28, 27, 27, 26), (31, 30, 30, 29)	Needle 1: Instep sts Needle 2: Sole sts Sts per needle: (19, 17), (25, 23), (31, 29), (37, 35), (43, 41), (49, 47), (55, 53), (61, 59)

Work toe decs as follows:		
4 dpn	5 dpn	2 circular needles
Rnd 1	**Rnd 1**	**Rnd 1**
Needle 1: K1, ssk, knit to last 3 sts, K2tog, K1.	Needle 1: K1, ssk, knit to end.	Needle 1: K1, ssk, knit to last 3 sts, K2tog, K1.
Needle 2: K1, ssk, knit to end.	Needle 2: Knit to last 3 sts, K2tog, K1.	Needle 2: K1, ssk, knit to last 3 sts, K2tog, K1.
Needle 3: Knit to last 3 sts, K2tog, K1.	Needle 3: K1, ssk, knit to end.	
	Needle 4: Knit to last 3 sts, K2tog, K1.	

Rnd 2: Knit around.

Rep rnds 1 and 2 until 20 (24, 32, 36, 44, 48, 56, 60) total sts rem. Sts for instep and sole are: (11, 9), (13, 11), (17, 15), (19, 17), (23, 21), (25, 23), (29, 27), (31, 29).

Rep rnd 1 only until 10 (10, 14, 18, 22, 22, 26, 30) total sts rem. There are 5 (5, 7, 9, 11, 11, 13, 15) sts each on sole and instep; last 2 dec will be on instep.

Place instep sts on 1 needle and sole sts on 2nd needle. Graft sts tog with kitchener st (page 79).

TEN-STITCH MOSAIC PATTERNS

Mosaic patterns are an easy way to do multicolor knitting because you knit with only one color at a time for two rounds. If you want a textured look, the second round is purled, and for a smoother appearance, you just knit both rounds. The mosaic fabric is not as elastic as plain knitting so you may want to knit the leg with a larger needle than the foot. These socks are worked with a ribbed foot to make the foot fit just right. The heels are worked in stripes or solid with heel stitch and a chain selvage. The toes are worked in stripes as well for some balance and fun.

SKILL LEVEL: EXPERIENCED ◼◼◼◼

Simulated Basket Weave sock made with Strickwear fingering-weight hand-dyed yarn from Strickwear.com (colors Black and Scarlet O'Hara) on size 1 needles with a gauge of 8¾ sts to 1".

T Pattern sock made with Jawoll Superwash from Lang (colors 88 Teal and 197 Sage) on size 1 needles with a gauge of 9 sts to 1".

Chevron pattern sock made with Meilenweit 6 fach from Lana Grossa (colors 37 Blue and 35 Yellow) on size 2 needles with a gauge of 7½ sts to 1".

MATERIALS

Gather materials for the socks you'd like to make and select the pattern you'd like to use.

DIRECTIONS

Select the number of sts to CO based on the gauge for your yarn and needles and the circumference of the intended foot.

SOCK STITCHES

Gauge sts/1"	Foot Circumference in Inches														
	5	5½	6	6½	7	7½	8	8½	9	9½	10	10½	11	11½	12
	Number of sts to CO														
5			30			40	40			50	50			60	60
5½		30			40			50				60	60		
6	30			40			50	50		60	60			70	70
6½			40			50			60			70	70		80
7		40			50			60			70		80	80	
7½				50			60			70		80			90
8	40		50			60		70	70		80		90	90	
8½				60						80		90		100	100
9		50		60			70		80		90		100		110
9½						70		80		90		100		110	
10	50		60		70		80		90		100		110		120

CUFF AND LEG

Using dark yarn and one of the COs beg on page 73, CO 30 (40, 50, 60, 70, 80, 90, 100, 110, 120) sts. Divide sts per needle as follows:

4 dpn	5 dpn (for 30-st sock, it is more efficient to knit leg on 3 needles rather than 4)	2 circular needles
(10, 10, 10), (10, 10, 20), (20, 20, 10), (20, 20, 20), (20, 20, 30), (20, 20, 40), (20, 30, 40), (20, 30, 50), (30, 30, 50), (30, 30, 60)	(10, 10, 10) (10, 10, 10, 10), (10, 10, 10, 20), (20, 10, 20, 10), (10, 20, 20, 20), (20, 20, 20, 20), (20, 20, 20, 30), (30, 20, 30, 20), (20, 30, 30, 30), (30, 30, 30, 30)	(10, 20), (20, 20), (20, 30), (30, 30), (30, 40), (40, 40), (40, 50), (50, 50), (50, 60), (60, 60)

Join, being careful not to twist sts. Work K1, P1 ribbing or ribbing of choice for 1½". Knit 1 rnd of dark. Beg leg patt of choice (pages 108–110) with light and work to desired leg length.

HEEL FLAP

Work heel, alternating 2 rows of dark and 2 rows of light on 15 (20, 25, 30, 35, 40, 45, 50, 55, 60) sts, beg with WS row and ending with RS row. Move 1 st from heel to instep as follows to balance patt on instep:

Needles 1 and 2: Instep sts Needle 3: Heel Sts	Needles 1 and 2: Instep sts Needle 3: Heel Sts	Needle 1: Instep sts Needle 2: Heel sts
(5, 10, 15), (10, 10, 20), (10, 15, 25), (15, 15, 30), (15, 20, 35), (20, 20, 40), (20, 25, 45), (25, 25, 50), (25, 30, 55), (30, 30, 60)	(5, 10, 15), (10, 10, 20), (10, 15, 25), (15, 15, 30), (15, 20, 35), (20, 20, 40), (20, 25, 45), (25, 25, 50), (25, 30, 55), (30, 30, 60)	15 (20, 25, 30, 35, 40, 45, 50, 55, 60)

Turn work to beg heel on WS row.

Row 1 (WS): With dark, K1, purl to last stitch, sl 1 wyif.

Row 2: With dark, K1, *sl 1 wyib, K1, rep from * to last 2 (1, 2, 1, 2, 1, 2, 1, 2, 1) st(s), sl 1 (0, 1, 0, 1, 0, 1, 0, 1, 0) wyib, sl 1 wyif.

Row 3: With light, K1, purl to last stitch, slip last st wyif.

Row 4: With light, K2, *sl 1 wyib, K1, rep from * to last 1 (2, 1, 2, 1, 2, 1, 2, 1) st(s), K1 (0, 1, 0, 1, 0, 1, 0, 1, 0), sl 1 wyif.

Rep rows 1–4 until you have 16 (20, 26, 30, 36, 40, 46, 50, 56, 60) heel-flap rows; the last row should be a RS row.

HEEL TURN

Use dark and work as follows:

Row 1 (WS): P9 (11, 14, 16, 19, 21, 24, 26, 29, 31), P2tog, P1, turn.

Row 2: Sl 1, K4 (3, 4, 3, 4, 3, 4, 3, 4, 3), ssk, K1, turn. Note that there will be a small gap between working sts that form heel turn and unworked heel sts.

Row 3: Sl 1, purl to within 1 st of gap, P2tog, P1, turn.

Row 4: Sl 1, knit to within 1 st of gap, ssk, K1, turn.

Rep rows 3 and 4, inc 1 additional knit or purl st after the sl 1 until all side sts are worked; end with completed row 4. There should be 9 (12, 15, 16, 19, 22, 25, 28, 29, 32) sts left on heel flap. When working rows 3 and 4, there may be no ending single st to work; some numbers don't work out.

For ease of instructions, beg of rnd is now at center of bottom of foot. The needles are renumbered at this point. Needle 1 is beg of rnd and holds all heel-turn sts.

GUSSET

4 dpn	5 dpn	2 circular needles
Combine instep sts onto needle 2.	Needles 2 and 3: Instep sts	Needle 1: Heel sts
		Needle 2: Instep sts

With RS facing you, needle 1, and dark only, PU and knit 8 (10, 13, 15, 18, 20, 23, 25, 28, 30) sts from side of heel flap. PU and knit 2 extra sts at top of gusset, then

4 dpn	5 dpn	2 circular needles
Needle 2: *P1, K3, P1, rep from * across instep.	Needles 2 and 3: *P1, K3, P1, rep from * across instep.	Cont with needle 1: PM, *P1, K3, P1, rep from * for 10 (10, 15, 15, 20, 20, 25, 25, 30, 30) sts.
Needle 3: PU and knit 2 extra sts at top of gusset, PU and knit 8 (10, 13, 15, 18, 20, 23, 25, 28, 30) sts from side of heel flap, K4 (6, 7, 8, 9, 11, 12, 14, 14, 16) from needle 1.	Needle 4: PU and knit 2 extra sts at top of gusset, PU and knit 8 (10, 13, 15, 18, 20, 23, 25, 28, 30) sts from side of heel flap, K4 (6, 7, 8, 9, 11, 12, 14, 14, 16) from needle 1.	Needle 2: *P1, K3, P1, rep from * across instep. Work rem instep sts, PM, PU and knit 2 extra sts at top of gusset, PU and knit 8 (10, 13, 15, 18, 20, 23, 25, 28, 30) sts from side of heel flap, K4 (6, 7, 8, 9, 11, 12, 14, 14, 16) from needle 1.
Sts per needle: (15, 15, 14), (18, 20, 18), (23, 25, 22), (25, 30, 25), (30, 35, 29), (33, 40, 33), (38, 45, 37), (41, 50, 41), (45, 55, 44), (48, 60, 48)	Sts per needle: (15, 5, 10, 14), (18, 10, 10, 18), (23, 10, 15, 22), (25, 15, 15, 25), (30, 15, 20, 29), (33, 20, 20, 33), (38, 20, 25, 37), (41, 25, 25, 41), (45, 25, 30, 44), (48, 30, 30, 48)	Sts per needle: (25, 19), (28, 28), (38, 32), (40, 40), (50, 44), (53, 53), (63, 57), (66, 66), (75, 69), (78, 78)

CLOSE GUSSET TOP

Beg of rnd for dec is at center of bottom of foot. The foot is knit in dark with a ribbed patt on instep. This will help make the sock fit more snugly than a completely St-st foot.

4 dpn	5 dpn	2 circular needles
Needle 1: Knit to last 2 sts, ssk.	Needle 1: Knit to last 2 sts, ssk.	Needle 1: Knit to 2 sts before marker, ssk, SM, *P1, K3, P1, rep from *.
Needle 2: *P1, K3, P1, rep from *.	Needles 2 and 3: *P1, K3, P1, rep from *.	Needle 2: Cont in rib patt, SM, K2tog, knit to end.
Needle 3: K2tog, knit to end.	Needle 4: K2tog, knit to end.	

GUSSET DECREASES

4 dpn	5 dpn	2 circular needles
Rnd 1	**Rnd 1**	**Rnd 1**
Needle 1: Knit to last 3 sts, K2tog, K1.	Needle 1: Knit to last 3 sts, K2tog, K1.	Needle 1: Knit to 3 sts before marker, K2tog, K1, SM, work est patt.
Needle 2: Work est patt.	Needles 2 and 3: Work est patt.	Needle 2: Work est patt to marker, SM, K1, ssk, knit to end.
Needle 3: K1, ssk, knit to end.	Needle 4: K1, ssk, knit to end.	

Rnd 2: Work in est patt on instep and in St st on sole.

Rep rnds 1and 2 until 30 (40, 50, 60, 70, 80, 90, 100, 110, 120) total sts rem.

FOOT

4 dpns	5 dpns	2 circular needles
Cont St st on needles 1 and 3, and est patt on needle 2 to desired heel-to-toe length.	Cont St st on needles 1 and 4, and est patt on needles 2 and 3 to desired heel-to-toe length.	Rearrange sts so instep sts are on needle 1 and sole sts are on needle 2. Markers are no longer needed. Cont est patt to desired heel-to-toe length.

TOE SHAPING

Knit sts on needle 1. Renumber needles. Needle 1: Instep sts Needles 2 and 3: Sole sts	Knit sts on needle 1. Renumber needles. Needles 1 and 2: Instep sts Needles 3 and 4: Sole sts	Needle 1: Instep sts Needle 2: Sole sts

Toe is worked in dark and light. Beg with dark and then alternate light and dark for entire toe.

Work toe decs as follows:

Rnd 1 Needle 1: K1, ssk, knit to last 3 sts, K2tog, K1. Needle 2: K1, ssk, knit to end. Needle 3: Knit to last 3 sts, K2tog, K1.	**Rnd 1** Needle 1: K1, ssk, knit to end. Needle 2: Knit to last 3 sts, K2tog, K1. Needle 3: K1, ssk, knit to end. Needle 4: Knit to last 3 sts, K2tog, K1.	**Rnd 1** Needle 1: K1, ssk, knit to last 3 sts, K2tog, K1. Needle 2: K1, ssk, knit to last 3 sts, K2tog, K1.

Rnd 2: Knit around.

Rep rnds 1 and 2 until 14 (20, 26, 28, 34, 40, 46, 48, 54, 60) total sts rem. There are 7 (10, 13, 14, 17, 20, 23, 24, 27, 30) sts each on instep and sole.

Rep rnd 1 only until 10 (12, 14, 16, 18, 20, 22, 24, 26, 32) total sts rem. There are 5 (6, 7, 8, 9, 10, 11, 12, 13, 16) sts each on sole and instep.

Place instep sts on 1 needle and sole sts on 2nd needle. Graft sts tog with kitchener st (page 79).

SOCK BASICS

To begin to understand how socks are constructed, pay attention to structure. If you're new to knitting socks, understanding sock structure may seem daunting. To make it easier, refer to the three examples that follow. I knit them using a different color for each section.

Top-down sock with heel flap

Cuff
Leg
Heel flap →
Heel turn →
Gusset and → beginning of bottom of foot
Foot
Toe

Top-up sock with heel flap

Cuff
Gusset and center back heel
Heel turn →
Heel flap →
Leg
Foot
Toe

Top-down sock with short-row heel

Cuff
Stockinette band leg and heel
Short → row heel
Leg
Foot
Toe

CUFFS

When starting a new pair of socks, you may just dive in and use your current favorite cast on and then work a K1, P1 or a K2, P2 rib. But we have more choices for fancy socks or more interesting knitting. There are seven different cast-on methods (see page 73). Some create a stretchy or more durable standard cast on, while others create a decorative edge before the rib, like a picot cast on or frilled edge.

Ribbing is an elastic and durable beginning for a sock. Often a simple rib is just fine, but you may want to knit it with two colors for a stranded or Mosaic patterned sock. Or for a very soft cuff, you can knit a stockinette hem. Most of the cuffs in this collection are simple ribs or derivatives of the pattern structure that will be knit on the leg. Before casting on, think a bit about the cuff, or knit a gauge swatch of the pattern you intend to use. Then while knitting and thinking about the pattern, swatch a unique ribbing to use when you cast on.

HEELS

There are two parts to a heel: the heel flap and the heel turn.

HEEL FLAPS

Heel flaps are typically worked back and forth for a number of rows equal to half of the number of stitches used for the sock. One popular pattern for the heel flap is the heel stitch. It is a slip-stitch pattern that creates a dense and durable fabric for an area of the sock that may wear out faster than others. There are also several other choices for heel fabric; the eye-of-partridge stitch is also a slipped-stitch fabric that more closely resembles stockinette stitch, or you can use stockinette-stitch fabric as short-row heels are constructed. If you have a pattern on the leg of the sock that you really like and are going to wear the socks with clogs or sandals, why not continue the pattern down the heel (as in the Sailor's Ribbing sock on page 21).

The following two patterns have a slipped stitch at the ends of the rows.

Heel St with German Chain Selvage	
Even Stitches in Heel Flap	Odd Stitches in Heel Flap
Row 1 (WS): K1, purl to last st, sl 1 wyif. **Row 2:** K1, *sl 1 wyib, K1, rep from * to last st, sl 1 wyif. Rep rows 1 and 2.	**Row 1 (WS):** K1, purl to last st, sl 1 wyif. **Row 2:** K1, *K1, sl 1 wyib, rep from * to last 2 sts, K1, sl 1 wyif. Rep rows 1 and 2.

Eye of Partridge with German Chain Selvage	
Even Stitches in Heel Flap	Odd Stitches in Heel Flap
Rows 1 and 3 (WS): K1, purl to last st, sl 1 wyif. **Row 2:** K1, *sl 1 wyib, K1, rep from * to last st, sl 1 wyif. **Row 4:** K1, *K1, sl 1 wyib, rep from * to last 2 sts, sl 1 wyib, sl 1 wyif. Rep rows 1–4.	**Rows 1 and 3 (WS):** K1, purl to last st, sl 1 wyif. **Row 2:** K1, *K1, sl 1 wyib, rep from * to last 2 sts, K1, sl 1 wyif. **Row 4:** K1, *sl 1 wyib, K1, rep from * to last 2 sts, sl 1 wyib, sl 1 wyif. Rep rows 1–4.

The following three patterns DO NOT have a slipped stitch at the ends of the rows.

Heel St with 3-st Garter Edge	
Even Stitches in Heel Flap	Odd Stitches in Heel Flap
Row 1 (WS): K3, purl to end. **Row 2:** P3, *sl 1 wyib, K1, rep from * to last 3 sts, K3. Rep rows 1 and 2.	**Row 1 (WS):** K3, purl to end. **Row 2:** P3, *K1, sl 1 wyib, rep from * to last 4 sts, K4. Rep rows 1 and 2.

Eye of Partridge with 3-st Garter Edge	
Even Stitches in Heel Flap	Odd Stitches in Heel Flap
Rows 1 and 3 (WS): K3, purl to end. **Row 2:** P3, *sl 1 wyib, K1, rep from * to last 3 sts, K3. **Row 4:** P3, *K1, sl 1 wyib, rep from * to last 3 sts, K3. Rep rows 1–4.	**Rows 1 and 3 (WS):** K3, purl to end. **Row 2:** P3, *K1, sl 1 wyib, rep from * to last 4 sts, K4. **Row 4:** P3, *sl 1 wyib, K1, rep from * to last 4 sts, sl 1, K3. Rep rows 1–4.

Heel Flap with Stockinette St or Continuation of Leg Pattern with 3-st Garter Edge	
Stockinette Heel	Leg Pattern Cont on Heel Flap
Row 1 (WS): K3, purl to end. **Row 2:** P3, knit to end. Rep rows 1 and 2.	**Row 1 (WS):** K3, work patt on next rnd to last 3 sts, P3. (Remember, first 3 sts are garter st; start patt on 4th st.) **Row 2:** P3, work patt to last 3 sts, K3. Rep rows 1 and 2.

Following are instructions for heel flaps with garter edges as well as German chain selvage, and shown for an even number as well as an odd number of heel stitches. Substitute these heel stitches in the pattern you are working, and get back to the instructions when it comes time for the heel turn. If you have used the German chain selvage, be sure to purl the first stitch in the first row of the heel turn.

The patterns are written with either a chain selvage or a garter selvage. My favorite way to work a chain selvage is to knit the first stitch of each heel-flap row and slip the last stitch as if to purl with the yarn in front. The advantage to this is that you are slipping the edge stitch and working it immediately following. This leaves less opportunity for that stitch to loosen up. If it is a little loose, tighten it up when working the first two stitches of the heel flap. The garter selvage is worked by knitting the last and first stitch of every row or by purling the first and last stitch of every row.

HEEL TURN

The heel turn is worked back and forth in what is referred to as short rows—rows that are worked short of the end, two stitches worked together and then turned and worked short of the next end, again working two stitches together. By working this way, you create the little triangular shape that turns the direction of the knitting, which is quite remarkable for such a little bit of knitting.

PICKING UP INTO A CHAIN SELVAGE

You have the choice of picking up both loops of the chain or just the outside loop of the chain. The fabric of the heel flap wants to curl under, so you need to unroll it to make sure you can see the whole selvage edge when you are working.

Picking up both loops of chain: Slip the needle under both loops of the chain and pick up a new stitch. This produces a neat edge and leaves the chain on the inside of the sock.

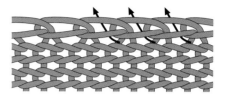

Picking up outside loop of chain: This creates a twisted, more-decorative stitch and leaves the inside of the sock the smoothest. Use a spare needle to pick up the outside loop and knit it through the back of the loop.

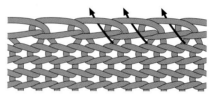

PICKING UP INTO A GARTER SELVAGE

This is perhaps the easiest way to work a heel flap and gusset. Pick up the thread between the garter bumps. You will be starting at a garter bump at the heel and beginning with the thread above the bump.

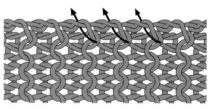

SHORT-ROW HEEL

All short-row procedures are the same regardless of the number of stitches you have reserved for the heel; the difference is the number of stitches remaining before you reverse short-row shaping. Refer to the pattern for the number of stitches in the heel and the number of stitches to be left unwrapped before you reverse short-row shaping.

Short-row leftover is about 40% of the stitches for the heel. If you have an even number of stitches in the heel, you will have an even number unworked. If odd, you will have an odd number remaining.

Before you start the heel, make a note of the pattern row you last worked, so it will be easy to remember where to start the pattern row when you begin working on the instep again.

BEGIN SHORT-ROW SHAPING

The instructions include a lot of markers. They help when reversing short rows to keep things lined up. You can use ring markers or make your own. I used Knit Cro Sheen yarn, but any smooth, contrasting yarn will work fine. Cut short lengths and tie a knot to make a small ring.

Row 1: Knit across heel sts to last 2 sts, yf, sl next st as if to purl, PM, yb, sl wrapped st pwise back to LH needle. Last st is unwrapped; 2nd st is wrapped on LH needle and remains unworked. Turn.

Row 2: Purl across row to last 2 sts, yb, sl next st as if to purl, PM, yf, sl wrapped st back to LH needle. Last st is unworked and unwrapped; 2nd st is wrapped and unworked. Turn.

Row 3: Knit across row to st before last wrapped st, yf, sl next st as if to purl, PM, yb, sl wrapped st back to LH needle. Turn.

Row 4: Purl across to st before last wrapped st, yb, sl next st, PM, yf, return slipped st to LH needle. Turn.

Rep rows 3 and 4 until the number of sts in the specific pattern you are knitting remain unwrapped. End ready for a RS row.

REVERSE SHORT-ROW SHAPING

Your short rows will be more attractive if you slip the wrap up and over the stitch before knitting it together with the stitch.

Row 1: Knit across to next wrapped st (st before first marker on left side). Knit st tog with wrap as follows: Remove marker, yf, sl next st as if to purl, yb, sl wrapped st back to LH needle. Turn. This stitch now has 2 wraps.

Row 2: Purl across to next wrapped st (st before first marker). Purl st tog with wrap as follows: Remove marker, sl st, place wrap on RH needle, sl both to LH needle as if to purl. Purl st tog with wrap through back loop (needle entering on back of work from left to right), yb, sl next st to RH needle, yf, return st to LH needle. Turn.

Row 3: Knit across to next wrapped st (st before next marker on left side). Knit st tog with both wraps as follows: Sl knit st to RH needle as if to purl, PU and knit wraps with LH needle and place on RH needle, sl all 3 sts back to LH needle as if to purl and K3tog. Drop marker, yf, sl next st as if to purl, yb, sl st back to LH needle. Turn.

Row 4: Purl to next wrapped st (st before next marker). Purl st tog with wrap as follows: Sl st to RH needle, PU and knit 2 wraps from base of st and place on RH needle over first st slipped, sl them back 1 at a time as if to purl to LH needle and P3tog through back loop. Wrap next st and drop marker. For rest of shaping, you will add a second wrap to each st.

Rep rows 3 and 4 until you have worked all wrapped sts. There is 1 marker on each side before first unwrapped st. When you have worked last wrapped st on RS, drop marker and wrap last st; turn and purl to last wrapped st on side. Purl wrapped stitch with its wraps as above; wrap last st. Turn.

The heel is now finished, and you have both end sts wrapped.

With heel-st yarn, knit across heel, knitting wrap with last st of heel. Work across instep; when you get back to heel sts, knit first heel st with wrap.

TOES

There are many ways to work the toes of a sock. I have used the standard toe in most cases as it works on the large range of sizes that are in most patterns. Below are directions for working four additional types of toes.

STAR TOE

You can see this toe in the Six-Stitch Stranded socks (page 52). The star toe uses the same decrease sequence as the standard toe. To work, decrease four times every other round until you have half the original number of stitches, then decrease four times every round until you have a quarter the original number of stitches or eight stitches, and then graft or thread a needle through the stitches and fasten off.

ROUND TOE

A round toe is beautiful, as can be seen in the Traveling Vine sock (page 37). But it can be problematic when working with a very few stitches and a great many stitches. It is worked with decreases evenly spaced around the toe, typically with eight decreases (or increases if you are working toe-up) per round. You work an ever-decreasing number (starting with six) of plain rounds between decrease rounds. With a 32-stitch sock, it works out that you only have a few rounds, not enough to cover the toes, and with an 80-stitch sock you would have to start the toe just about as you finish the gusset. For working round toes on very small or very large numbers of stitches, you need to do some math to figure out how many rows you need. I have done the math and included numbers for a few midrange numbers of stitches.

Top-Down Socks

Place markers or arrange to be at end of needle every 6 (7, 8, 9) stitches.

48-Stitch Sock

*Knit to 2 sts before marker or end of needle, K2tog, rep from *—40 sts.

Knit 5 rnds.

*Knit to 2 sts before marker or end of needle, K2tog, rep from *—32 sts.

Knit 3 rnds.

*Knit to 2 sts before marker or end of needle, K2tog, rep from *—16 sts.

Knit 2 rnds.

*Knit to 2 sts before marker or end of needle, K2tog, rep from *—8 sts.

Break yarn and thread tail through the 8 sts and weave in on inside of sock.

56-Stitch Sock

*Knit to 2 sts before marker or end of needle, K2tog, rep from *—48 sts.

Knit 5 rnds.

*Knit to 2 sts before marker or end of needle, K2tog, rep from *—40 sts.

Knit 4 rnds.

*Knit to 2 sts before marker or end of needle, K2tog, rep from *—32 sts.

Knit 3 rnds.

*Knit to 2 sts before marker or end of needle, K2tog, rep from *—24 sts.

Knit 2 rnds.

*Knit to 2 sts before marker or end of needle, K2tog, rep from *—16 sts.

Knit 1 rnd.

*Knit to 2 sts before marker or end of needle, K2tog, rep from *—8 sts.

Break yarn and thread tail through the 8 sts and weave in on inside of sock.

64-Stitch Sock

*Knit to 2 sts before marker or end of needle, K2tog, rep from *—56 sts.

Knit 5 rnds.

*Knit to 2 sts before marker or end of needle, K2tog, rep from *—48 sts.

Knit 4 rnds.

*Knit to 2 sts before marker or end of needle, K2tog, rep from *—40 sts.

Knit 3 rnds.

*Knit to 2 sts before marker or end of needle, K2tog, rep from *—32 sts.

Knit 2 rnds.

*Knit to 2 sts before marker or end of needle, K2tog, rep from *—24 sts.

Knit 1 rnd.

*Knit to 2 sts before marker or end of needle, K2tog, rep from * twice—8 sts.

Break yarn and thread tail through the 8 sts and weave in on inside of sock.

72-Stitch Sock
*Knit to 2 sts before marker or end of needle, K2tog, rep from *—64 sts.

Knit 5 rnds.

*Knit to 2 sts before marker or end of needle, K2tog, rep from *—56 sts.

Knit 4 rnds.

*Knit to 2 sts before marker or end of needle, K2tog, rep from *—48 sts.

Knit 3 rnds.

*Knit to 2 sts before marker or end of needle, K2tog, rep from *—40 sts.

Knit 2 rnds.

*Knit to 2 sts before marker or end of needle, K2tog, rep from *—32 sts.

Knit 2 rnds.

*Knit to 2 sts before marker or end of needle, K2tog, rep from * 3 times—8 sts.

Break yarn and thread tail through the 8 sts and weave in on inside of sock.

Toe-Up Socks

48-Stitch Sock
*M1, K1, rep from *—16 sts.

Knit 1 rnd.

*M1, K2, rep from *—24 sts.

Knit 2 rnds.

*M1, K3, rep from *—32 sts.

Knit 3 rnds.

*M1, K4, rep from *—40 sts.

Knit 3 rnds.

*M1, K5, rep from *—48 sts.

Knit 5 rnds.

56-Stitch Sock
*M1, K1, rep from *—16 sts.

Knit 1 rnd.

*M1, K2, rep from *—24 sts.

Knit 2 rnds.

*M1, K3, rep from *—32 sts.

Knit 3 rnds.

*M1, K4, rep from *—40 sts.

Knit 4 rnds.

*M1, K5, rep from *—48 sts.

Knit 5 rnds.

*M1, K6, rep from *—56 sts.

Knit 3 rnds.

64-Stitch Sock
*M1, K1, rep from *—16 sts.

*M1, K2, rep from *—24 sts.

Knit 1 rnd.

*M1, K3, rep from *—32 sts.

Knit 2 rnds.

*M1, K4, rep from *—40 sts.

Knit 3 rnds.

*M1, K5, rep from *—48 sts.

Knit 4 rnds.

*M1, K6, rep from *—56 sts.

Knit 5 rnds.

*M1, K7, rep from *—64 sts.

Knit 3 rnds.

72-Stitch Sock
*M1, K1, rep from *—16 sts.

*M1, K2, rep from *—24 sts.

Knit 1 rnd.

*M1, K3, rep from *—32 sts.

Knit 2 rnds.

*M1, K4, rep from *—40 sts.

Knit 2 rnds.

*M1, K5, rep from *—48 sts.

Knit 3 rnds.

*M1, K6, rep from *—56 sts.

Knit 4 rnds.

*M1, K7, rep from *—64 sts.

Knit 5 rnds.

*M1, K8, rep from *—72 sts.

Knit 3 rnds.

THE SIX-GORE TOE

My friend Beth Parrott used this toe when she knit the Komi Vine sock (page 57), and it got me thinking and figuring. This works on socks with cast on of 30, 36, 42, 48, 54, 60, 66, 72, 78, 84, 90, 96, 102, 108, 114, 120 stitches. To work, decrease six times evenly on every other round until you have six stitches left. This will yield a toe of 8, 10, 12, 14, 16, 18, 20, 22, 24, 26, 28, 30, 32, 34, 36, 38 rounds. This is a simple method and yields the same number of rounds (within 3) as when working a standard toe.

MITTEN TOE WITH PINSTRIPING

When working a pinstripe pattern on the sole, such as in the Heart Crook tessellated sock on page 57, it is fun to continue the pinstriping on the toe. But managing the stripes in a seamless manner takes some thought and finesse to finish and have all the stripes continue. Here is a method that works to preserve the pinstripe integrity.

For the tessellated sock, you have two more stitches on the instep than on the sole. The instructions below indicate what to do with the knitting, but you need to keep track of the colors you are working. Begin the decreases on the instep side.

Rnd 1: (Instep) K1, ssk, knit to last 3 sts, K2tog, K1. (Sole) Ssk, knit to last 2 sts, K2tog.

At this point, the top and bottom will be bordered by the same color pinstripe, with the stitch on either side of the instep as the solid border between them.

Rnd 2: Work pinstripe colors as they appear on the needles.

Rep rnds 1 and 2 until 20 (24, 32, 36, 44, 48, 56, 60) sts remain.

Working in stranded, Fair Isle-type knitting produces stitches that are taller than stockinette stitches; if you have short toes you may want to stop working the plain rounds sooner (working just decrease rounds) to have a toe that is less pointy; however, if you have pointy toes, this sequence may suit you.

Cont working rnd 1 until 8 stitches remain: 5 on the instep and 3 on the sole. Starting with the instep and working in color, K1, sl 2, K1, p2sso, K1. Now rearrange the stitches so that instead of instep and sole you have right and left sides; they should match so that you have a dark, light, dark or light, dark, light on each needle. Now graft the two sets of stitches together.

KNITTING TECHNIQUES

Basic long-tail cast on

Long-tail cast on in K2, P2 ribbing

Twisted German cast on

Two-color cast on with corrugated ribbing

Picot cast on

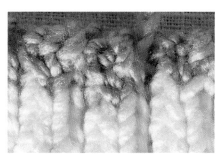

Frilled cast on

Hemmed top

CAST ONS

Seven different cast-on methods are used for the socks in this book: a variety of long-tail cast ons for top-down socks, a provisional cast on for the easy toe for toe-up socks, and a knit-on cast on to use for picot cast on as well as when you want to begin your socks with a hem. If you take some time to try a new cast on, you will be rewarded with a more suitable beginning for your knitting as well as an expanded set of knitting skills.

CAST ONS FOR TOP-DOWN SOCKS

Long-Tail Cast On

Most knitters are familiar with the basic long-tail cast on. I've provided a few variations of the basic method that work well with socks.

Basic long-tail cast on. The long-tail cast on is elastic and sturdy. Use this technique when casting on for a sock that begins with ribbing. To work the long-tail cast on, make a slipknot with a tail about four times the length of the sock circumference. Place the slipknot on the right-hand needle. Hold both lengths of yarn in the left hand, with the tail over the thumb and the long end over the index finger. Both ends are tensioned by holding them in the palm with the other fingers (fig. 1). Insert the right-hand needle into the front of the loop on the thumb and over the yarn on the index finger (fig. 2). Bring this yarn through the loop on the thumb (fig. 3), forming a loop on the needle; tighten gently by placing the thumb under the yarn now coming from the needle and gently pulling back on it. This same motion sets up the loop on the thumb for the next stitch. Repeat for the required number of stitches.

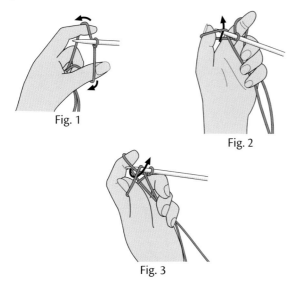

Fig. 1

Fig. 2

Fig. 3

Long-tail cast on for purl. The basic long-tail cast on essentially produces a knit stitch. However, you can also work a long-tail cast on as a purl. When you cast on in this manner for K1, P1 or K2, P2 ribbing, the cast-on edge becomes almost invisible, as the cast-on purled stitches recede into the purl stitches of the ribbing.

To cast on in purl, begin as for the regular long-tail cast on, but treat the loop on the thumb like a stitch on the left-hand needle, and the yarn around the index finger like the yarn on a continental knitter's left finger when knitting. The motion of the needle and yarn is the same as making a purl stitch. Bring the needle behind the front strands of both loops (fig. 1). Catch the index-finger loop (fig. 2) and draw it through the thumb loop to complete the purl cast on (fig. 3). Repeat for the required number of stitches.

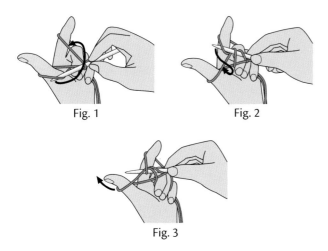

Fig. 1

Fig. 2

Fig. 3

Working the knits and purls in the cast on gives you the option to work knit and purl sequences other than K1, P1 and K2, P2, such as for a five-stitch ribbing pattern like K1, P1, K1, P2.

Twisted German Cast On

This method provides more elasticity than the regular long-tail cast on. Begin as in basic long-tail cast on. Put the needle under both loops of the thumb yarn (fig. 1), pointing it toward the index finger. Bring the needle back into the loop just below the thumb and up toward you (fig. 2). Bend your thumb toward the index finger, and scoop the index-finger yarn back through the twisted loop (the loop that you just opened by bending your thumb) (fig. 3). The yarn from the index finger is now on the needle. Drop the thumb loop off the thumb (fig. 4). Snug the yarns up against the needle. Repeat for the required number of stitches.

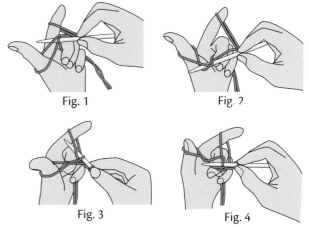

Fig. 1

Fig. 2

Fig. 3

Fig. 4

Two-Color Cast On

This is useful when working a corrugated ribbing. Make a slipknot near the end of the yarn of each color and place the yarns on the needle. These two stitches do not count toward the number of stitches you need to cast on; they will be dropped off the needle after the stitches are cast on. Hold the yarn as for the basic long-tail cast on, with the main color over the thumb and the contrasting color over the index finger. Work as for the basic long-tail cast on.

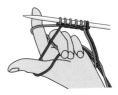

Knitted Cast Ons

The basic knitted cast on below is a very loose and unsubstantial cast on and should not be used alone for socks. It works well when used as part of another cast on such as a picot cast on, a frilled cast on, or a hem at the top of the cuff.

Basic Knitted Cast On. To work, make a slipknot and place it on the left-hand needle. Insert the right-hand needle into the loop and knit a stitch (fig. 1), then place the new stitch on the left-hand needle (fig. 2). I like to place the new stitch on the left-hand needle as if to knit, which means that both needles are in the loop with the points up. If you work in this manner, you can just tighten up on the stitch and start working the next stitch. You now have two stitches on the left-hand needle. *Knit into the next stitch on the left-hand needle and place the stitch on the right-hand needle. Repeat from * until you have the desired number of stitches.

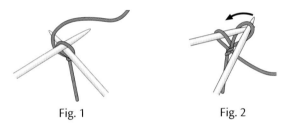

Fig. 1   Fig. 2

Picot Cast On. Cast on four stitches using the "Basic Knitted Cast On" described above, *K2, BO 1 st, K1, BO 1 (large picot made), place remaining stitch that is on right-hand needle back onto left-hand needle as if to purl. Cast on six stitches, repeat from * for desired number of stitches, end by placing remaining stitch that is on right-hand needle back on left-hand needle. Repeat from * until you have the desired number of stitches.

Frilled Cast On. This is a *guaranteed* nonbinding top. Cast on twice the number of stitches called for in the pattern, using the "Basic Knitted Cast On." Work two stitches together all the way around so that when you start the second round you will have the exact number of stitches you need for your sock. For example, for K2, P2 ribbing and a 48-stitch sock, cast on 96 stitches. **Rnd 1:** *K2tog, K2tog, P2tog, P2tog, rep from *. **Rnd 2:** *K2, P2, rep from *. Then continue with your cuff to the desired length.

Hemmed Top. A hem provides a nonbinding cast on to the top of a sock. Cast on the total number of stitches you need for the sock using the "Basic Knitted Cast On." Join, being careful not to twist the stitches. Work about ¾" of stockinette stitch. (Make a note of how many rounds you worked.) Work one round of picot pattern as follows: *YO, K2tog, rep from * to end. Work the same number of rounds as worked for the ¾". Join the hem as follows: with an extra double-pointed needle, pick up one stitch along the cast-on edge for every stitch cast on, then knit each stitch with its corresponding live stitch. It may be easier for you to pick up one stitch at a time, depending on the weight of the yarn.

CAST ONS FOR TOE-UP SOCKS

Loop-de-Loop Cast On

This cast on is easy and works beautifully when working a toe-up sock with a round toe.

1. Make a ring of yarn 1½" in diameter, and then pull the tail through the ring, back to front and left to right (fig. 1).

2. Put the needle under the working yarn and pull up a loop (this mimics a yarn over)—one stitch cast on (fig. 2).

3. With the working yarn behind the ring, put the point of the needle through the ring from front to back (fig. 3).

4. Put the needle over the working yarn and pull up a loop through the ring—second stitch cast on. Do not pull the yarn tightly; leave the ring open (fig. 4).

Repeat steps 2–4 for the desired number of stitches, always ending with step 4. After knitting the first row, pull the tail to tighten the stitches. Without turning the needle, push the stitches to the right-hand point. Pull the working yarn from left to right (as with I-cord) and knit the stitches through the back of the loop.

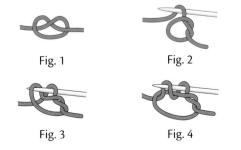

Fig. 1   Fig. 2

Fig. 3   Fig. 4

Provisional Cast On

This technique is used when casting on for a toe-up sock or when you need to pick up stitches from the cast on so that you can knit in the opposite direction. This cast on provides very little bulk so that after you pick up and knit in the opposite direction, the join is undetectable. The waste yarn is easiest to take out after the stitches have been picked up.

Work with waste yarn, a double-pointed needle in your left hand, and a crochet hook with a slipknot in your right hand. Place the double-pointed needle over the long strand held in your left hand. With the hook, draw a loop over the needle and through the slipknot. Place the yarn under the needle again, *with the hook, draw a loop over the needle and through the stitch on the hook, rep from * until you have one stitch less than the number required. Transfer the last loop from the crochet hook to the needle after you have moved the yarn to the back of the needle. Cut the waste yarn and begin knitting with sock yarn. To remove the chain, unravel the crochet chain, placing each stitch on the needle.

DECREASES

When knitting a gusset, the decreases are paired along the sides of the foot. You will use different decrease methods for the left and right sides of the foot.

RIGHT-SLANTING DECREASE

I recommend the "knit two together (K2tog)" for the right-slanting decrease because it yields such beautiful results. This decrease is typically used on the left side of the knitted fabric. Knit two stitches together through the front loops as one stitch. The decreased stitches will line up beautifully.

LEFT-SLANTING DECREASE

This decrease is typically used on the right side of the knitted fabric. There are a number of ways that knitters can make this decrease, although none of them look as beautiful as the K2tog when they are worked. After the knitting is washed, they all look better, but still not as nice as the K2tog. In the text, I have indicated ssk for a left-leaning decrease. You may substitute sl l, Kl, psso; however, I would advise that you choose one and stick with it for consistency in the look of the sock.

Slip, slip, knit (ssk): Slip the first and second stitches, one at a time, as if to knit, then insert the point of the left-hand needle into the fronts of these two stitches, and knit them together from this position. Some knitters slip the first stitch as if to knit and the second one as if to purl because they like the appearance of this method better.

Slip one, knit one, pass slipped stitch over (sl 1, K1, psso): Slip one stitch as if to purl with the yarn in back, knit the next stitch, then pass the slipped stitch over the knit stitch and off the needle.

INCREASES

There are many ways to increase, but the following are used in this book.

MAKE ONE (M1)

Insert left-hand needle from back to front under the horizontal strand between the last stitch and the next stitch, and knit into the front of the stitch to twist it closed.

MAKE ONE REVERSED (M1R)

Insert left-hand needle from front to back under the horizontal strand between the last stitch and the next stitch, and knit into the back of the stitch to twist it closed.

KNIT ONE INTO FRONT AND BACK (K1F&B)

Knit into the front and back of the same stitch. You have one more stitch on the needle.

BIND OFFS FOR TOE-UP SOCKS

Standard bind off

Suspended bind off

Decrease bind off

Frilled bind off

Picot bind off

Kitchener bind off for K1, P1

Kitchener bind off for K2, P2

These bind-off techniques are used at the top of the cuff when working a sock from the toe up. Just as you want a cast on for top-down socks that is loose and elastic, the bind off needs to be at least as elastic as the fabric and the same size. Some look similar to the standard bind off and some are decorative. Try one of the alternatives in a swatch to see what works for you.

STANDARD BIND OFF

Work two stitches; with the left-hand needle, pull the first stitch over the second stitch and off the needle. *Work another stitch and pull the previous one over it. Repeat from * to end.

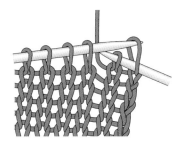

SUSPENDED BIND OFF

This bind off helps keep the stitches even on the bound-off edge. It also keeps the edge from becoming too tight or the stitches from stretching unevenly. Begin as for the standard bind off, but keep the lifted stitch on the left-hand needle and then work the next stitch on the left-hand needle. Then slip off both the suspended stitch and new stitch together in one movement. This will leave two stitches on the right-hand needle. Draw the first stitch over the second and retain on the left-hand needle as before. Continue to end.

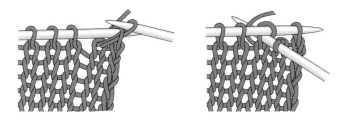

DECREASE BIND OFF

This produces another even bound-off edge. Knit the first stitch. *Slip the next stitch knitwise, insert the left needle into the front of the two stitches on the right needle and knit the two stitches together. One stitch remains on the right-hand needle. Repeat from * to end.

FRILLED BIND OFF

This bind off doubles the number of stitches during the bind-off round, making a very loose or frilled edge. To bind off, work the first stitch, M1, bind off the first stitch. *Work the next stitch on the left-hand needle, bind off, M1, bind off. Repeat from * to end.

PICOT BIND OFF

This bind off adds elasticity to the bound-off edge without the picots being very visible: *Cast on 1 stitch, using the "Basic Knitted Cast On" (see page 75); bind off three stitches, using the standard bind off, place the remaining stitch that is on the right-hand needle back on the left-hand needle and repeat from * to end.

KITCHENER STITCH BIND OFF FOR K1, P1 RIBBING

This bind off makes a nice finished edge on ribbing that is more attractive than the standard bind off. Using two circular or double-pointed needles, depending on the number of stitches you have, separate the knit stitches from the purl stitches. As the stitches face you, insert one needle into the first knit stitch, the second needle into the purl stitch, and repeat across. Half the stitches will be on one needle and half will be on the second needle. When you look at the knitting on either side, there will be knit stitches on the needle facing you.

Cut the working yarn about three times the width of the knitting plus about 12" extra to weave in. Thread the yarn through a yarn needle. You will direct the yarn needle as if it were a knitting needle, working the two pieces together, on knitting needles held in the left hand.

1. Go through the first stitch on the front needle as if to purl. Leave stitch on needle.
2. Go through first stitch on back needle as if to knit. Leave stitch on needle. Keep the yarn between the needles so it is not mistaken for another stitch. Adjust tension as you work.
3. *Go through the first stitch on front needle as if to knit, and through the next stitch on front needle as if to purl. Drop off first stitch on front needle.
4. Go through first stitch on back needle as if to purl, and through next stitch on back needle as if to knit. Drop off first stitch on back needle*. Repeat from * to * until there is one stitch on each needle.
5. Go through remaining stitch on front needle as if to knit and drop stitch off.
6. Go through remaining stitch on back needle as if to purl and drop stitch off. Finish by weaving in end.

Here is a shortcut to help you remember what to do:

Front needle: Knit off, purl on.

Back needle: Purl off, knit on.

You can also use the above kitchener bind off on K2, P2 ribbing. For a more balanced and seamless bind off, unknit the first knit stitch and place it on the previous needle; this will be the last stitch grafted off. Start with a K1 on the front needle, then P2 on the back needle, and then continue with K2 on front, P2 on back, and so on, ending with a K1. Work as for binding off K1, P1 ribbing.

SEWING TOES TOGETHER WITH KITCHENER STITCH

Use the kitchener stitch to sew the ends of the toes together. Work with the two pieces on the needles with wrong sides together, one needle behind the other. Thread a yarn needle with the yarn attached to the back needle and follow steps 1–6 on page 78.

TROUBLESHOOTING

You can avoid the problems that often plague sock knitting by using a few simple techniques.

AVOIDING EARS ON HEEL TURN

As careful as I was about picking up stitches for the gusset, I would sometimes notice a little ear at one side of the heel turn. In thinking about the way most socks are knit, I realized that there is one extra row worked after the heel is turned. If you are working with heavier yarn, this extra row would account for the ear. So I tried completing the heel turn on a right-side row, eliminating the need to work a plain knit row before picking up gusset stitches. I eliminated the ear! This way of working is not standard and for those of you who reflexively knit that way, pay attention to the instructions; all the heel flaps start on a wrong-side row because you turn first, not after the first row has been worked.

AVOIDING GAP AT TOP OF GUSSET

The hole or gap at the top of the gusset is a perennial problem for sock knitters. Some instructions do not provide any suggestion for how to alleviate this situation and some suggest picking up one stitch, without any specifics on exactly where or how to do this.

I like to pick up two extra stitches at the top of the gusset. The way to identify these stitches is to look for the horizontal thread between the first instep stitch and the heel-flap stitch. Insert the needle into the left half of the heel-flap stitch and pick up one stitch; then pick up the right half of the first instep stitch from the row below the stitch on the needle. Both of these stitches are on the gusset needle.

When picking up the gusset on the other side of the sock, again locate the horizontal thread between the instep and heel flap; pick up the outside halves of each stitch and place on the needle you will use for the heel gusset. If these stitches have been purled, just pick up through the purl bump. These two extra stitches are worked together on the first gusset round.

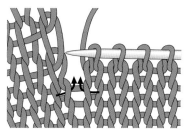

Picking up stitches when both were knit

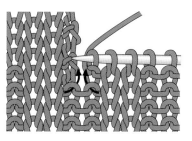

Picking up stitches when both were purled

AVOIDING EARS ON THE ENDS OF A KITCHENER-GRAFTED TOE

The last few stitches that are worked when you graft the toe may become slightly stretched and may seem larger than the ones in the middle. To avoid this, I work the kitchener grafting rather tightly, and when finished, take the yarn with the needle and thread it into the space between the last two stitches grafted together. Then I weave in the end on the inside of the sock.

SMALL JOG AT CAST-ON EDGE OF CUFF

One way to even the cast-on round is to take the tail from the cast on and work it between the first and last stitches to even them out. Another alternative is to cast on one extra stitch. As you are working the first round, work the first stitch and the last stitch together as follows: slip the last stitch, work the first (first stitch or round 2), and pass the last stitch over the first.

PICKING COLORS FOR MULTIPLE YARN SOCKS

One way to create colorful socks is to use one solid-colored yarn and one hand-painted yarn. For clear reading of the pattern, make sure that the solid-colored yarn is either darker than the darkest color in the hand-painted yarn, or lighter than the lightest. If you are working with all solids, try a swatch if you have a light and dark of the same hue; they may not contrast as much in the knitting as they do when you hold the two skeins next to one another. The farther apart the colors are on the color wheel the more contrast you will have.

When selecting yarns for the tessellated patterns, a wide range of colors are more eye-catching. To create balance, try to pick warm as well as cool colors. If there are many bright, clear colors and one dull color such as a gray, the dull color will get lost in the pattern. Again, a small swatch will inform you if any individual yarns are not working before you start the sock.

ADDING NEW YARN

Most of the time the skeins of yarn will be enough to knit one sock. However, if you're using leftovers, knitting stripes, or you've run out and are adding new yarn, this method works well for socks as well as for most other knitting projects. Stop knitting when there is a tail of at least 4", and then lay the new yarn alongside the old yarn and knit the next two stitches with both yarns held together. Be sure to leave a 4" tail on the new yarn. Drop the old yarn, leaving a 4" tail, and continue with the new yarn. After you knit past this addition, tighten the stitches by pulling on the tails. Even with very fine or very bulky yarn, tugging on the tails will not make a thick spot in the knitting. When you are finished, use a darning needle and weave the ends in. This is secure, and the stitches will not work themselves out.

CAST ON IS TOO TIGHT

If you are using a long-tail-type cast on, it is easy to get into a rhythm and move quickly and very tightly. Try to take your time and concentrate on keeping the final step of the cast on loose. Casting on over two needles only makes the first row of stitches loose; the base of the cast on may still be too tight and not solve the situation.

TABLES

The tables in this section provide information on gauge and needle size, how much yardage you need to make socks, and standard foot measurements for children, women, and men.

GAUGE AND NEEDLE SIZE

To get the most accurate gauge swatch, you should knit the swatch in the round, using the pattern for the sock you want to make. But I have found that for all but cable socks, you can knit a swatch back and forth in stockinette stitch to get a good idea of your gauge. Remember to wash and block the swatch before measuring it.

When working with a new yarn, I knit a flat swatch of at least 30 stitches and knit for about 4" in stockinette stitch. I try several different needle sizes to get a feel for the fabric that I want for the sole of my foot. I then measure the portion of the stockinette-stitch fabric that I like the best to determine the gauge. All of the gauge numbers refer to stockinette stitch and accommodate the texture patterns of the socks.

SUGGESTED GAUGE AND NEEDLE SIZE		
Yarn Weight	Stitch Gauge per Inch	Needle Size
Fingering	8½ to 10 sts	U.S. 0 (2.0 mm) or 1 (2.25 mm)
Sport	7½ to 9 sts	U.S. 2 (2.5 mm)
DK	6½ to 8 sts	U.S. 3 (3.25 mm)
Worsted	6 to 7 sts	U.S. 4 (3.5 mm)

YARDAGE YIELDS

The following table indicates the approximate number of yards you can expect to find in 50-gram and 100-gram skeins or balls of yarn.

YARDAGE YIELDS		
Yarn Weight	Yards per 50 g	Yards per 100 g
Fingering	180 to 230	360 to 460
Sport	150 to 180	300 to 360
DK	120 to 145	240 to 290
Worsted	100 to 110	200 to 220

HOW MUCH YARN DOES IT TAKE TO KNIT A PAIR OF SOCKS?

It depends on the weight of the yarn, the size needles you are using, the size of the foot you are knitting for, and the density of the fabric you are creating. Below is a chart of approximate yardage for socks.

APPROXIMATE YARDS NEEDED FOR A PAIR OF SOCKS				
Yarn Weight	Children (Small)	Children (Medium)	Women	Men
Fingering	275	340	430	525
Sport	215	275	370	430
DK	200	250	340	400
Worsted	185	215	310	370

FOOT MEASUREMENTS AND SIZES

It is helpful to know the foot circumference, the length of the foot, the height of the leg you want to knit, and the height of the heel. If the socks are for you, it is easy to measure your bare foot. If you cannot measure the recipient's foot, I have included charts for children, women, and men based on shoe size.

SIZE CHART FOR CHILDREN						
Shoe Size	Foot Circumference in Inches	Sock Length in Inches				
		Leg	Heel Flap	Heel to Toe	Toe	Total Foot
4	5	2⅞	1⅜	3⅜	⅞	4¼
5	5¼	3¼	1⅜	3½	1¼	4¾
6	5½	3¼	1¾	3¾	1¼	5
7	5¾	3⅝	1¾	4	1¼	5¼
8	6¼	3¾	1⅞	4¾	1¼	5½
9	6¼	4⅛	1⅞	4¾	1¼	6
10	6¾	4⅜	1⅞	4¾	1½	6¼
11	6¾	4¾	2	5⅛	1⅝	6¾
12	6¾	5	2	5⅜	1⅝	7
13	7	5¼	2	5¾	1⅝	7⅜

SIZE CHART FOR WOMEN								
Shoe Size	Foot Circumference in Inches			Sock Length in Inches				
	Narrow	Medium	Wide	Leg	Heel Flap	Heel to Toe	Toe	Total Foot
5	6⅝	7½	8⅜	6⅛	2	7⅛	1⅝	8¾
5½	6¾	7⅝	8½	6¼	2	7¼	1⅝	8⅞
6	6⅞	7¾	8¾	6¼	2⅛	7¼	1¾	9
6½	7⅛	7⅞	8¾	6½	2⅛	7½	1¾	9¼
7	7¼	8⅛	9	6½	2¼	7⅝	1¾	9⅜
7½	7¼	8¼	9⅛	6¾	2¼	7¾	1¾	9½
8	7½	8⅜	9¼	6¾	2¼	8	1¾	9¾
8½	7⅝	8½	9⅜	6⅞	2¼	8	1¾	9¾
9	7¾	8¾	9½	7	2¼	8	2	10
9½	7⅞	8¾	9¾	7¼	2¼	8¼	2	10¼
10	8⅛	9	9¾	7¼	2¼	8¼	2	10¼
10½	8¼	9⅛	10	7⅜	2⅜	8½	2	10½
11	8⅜	9¼	10⅛	7⅝	2⅜	8¾	2	10¾
11½	8½	9⅜	10¼	7¾	2⅜	8¾	2	10¾
12	8¾	9½	10⅜	7⅞	2⅜	9	2	11

SIZE CHART FOR MEN							
Shoe Size	Foot Circumference in Inches			Sock Length in Inches				
	Narrow	Medium	Wide	Leg	Heel Flap	Heel to Toe	Toe	Total Foot
6	7¼	8¼	9⅛	6½	2⅛	7⅝	1¾	9⅜
6½	7½	8⅜	9¼	6¾	2⅛	7¾	1⅞	9½
7	7⅝	8½	9⅜	6¾	2¼	7¾	2	9¾
7½	7¾	8¾	9½	6⅞	2¼	7¾	2	9¾
8	7⅞	8¾	9¾	7	2¼	8	2	10
8½	8⅛	9	9¾	7⅛	2¼	8¼	2	10¼
9	8¼	9⅛	10	7¼	2¼	8¼	2	10¼
9½	8⅜	9¼	10⅛	7⅜	2⅜	8½	2⅛	10⅝
10	8½	9⅜	10¼	7½	2⅜	8⅝	2⅛	10¾
10½	8¾	9½	10⅜	7⅝	2⅜	8¾	2⅛	10⅞
11	8¾	9¾	10⅝	7¾	2½	8⅞	2⅛	11
11½	9	9¾	10¾	7¾	2½	8⅞	2¼	11⅛
12	9⅛	10	10⅞	7⅞	2⅝	8⅞	2⅜	11¼
12½	9¼	10⅛	11	8⅛	2⅝	9⅛	2⅜	11½
13	9¾	10¼	11¼	8¼	2⅝	9¼	2⅜	11⅝
13½	9½	10⅜	11¼	8¼	2¾	9⅜	2⅜	11¾
14	9¾	10⅝	11½	8⅜	2¾	9⅝	2⅜	12
14½	9¾	10¾	11⅝	8⅝	2¾	9¾	2⅜	12⅛
15	10	10⅞	11¾	8¾	2¾	9⅞	2⅜	12¼

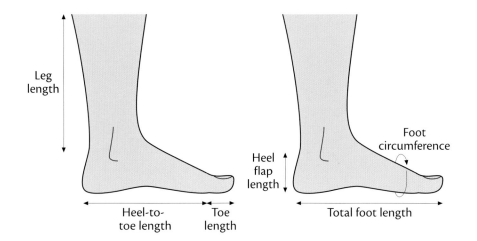

Leg length · Heel-to-toe length · Toe length · Heel flap length · Foot circumference · Total foot length

ABBREVIATIONS AND GLOSSARY

approx	approximately	rnd(s)	round(s)
beg	begin(ning)	RS	right side
BO	bind off	sl	slip
cn	cable needle	sl 1	slip one stitch purlwise with yarn in back unless otherwise noted
CO	cast on		
cont	continue, continuing	sl 1, K1, psso	slip one stitch, knit one stitch, pass slipped stitch over (see page 76)
dec(s)	decrease(s), decreasing		
dpn	double-pointed needles	SM	slip marker
est	established	ssk	slip one stitch, slip one stitch, knit the two stitches together (see page 76)
foll	following		
g	gram		
inc(s)	increase(s), increasing	st(s)	stitch(es)
K	knit	St st	stockinette stitch
K1-b	knit one stitch through back loop	tog	together
K1f&b	knit into front and back of same stitch (see page 76)	TW2R	knit two stitches together, leave stitches on left needle, knit first stitch and slip both stitches off needle
K2tog	knit two stitches together (see page 76)		
kw	knitwise		
LH	left hand	WS	wrong side
M1	make one stitch (see page 76)	wyib	with yarn in back
M1R	make one stitch reversed (see page 76)	wyif	with yarn in front
		yb	yarn back
MC	main color	yds	yards
P	purl	yf	yarn forward
patt(s)	pattern(s)	YO	yarn over
PM	place marker		
psso	pass slipped stitch over		
p2sso	pass two slipped stitches over		
PU	pick up		
pw	purlwise		
rem	remain, remaining		
rep(s)	repeat(s)		
RH	right hand		

SKILL LEVELS

■□□□
Beginner

■■□□
Easy

■■■□
Intermediate

■■■■
Experienced

STITCH DICTIONARY

The stitch dictionary is divided into patterns for each sock chapter in the book. Within some of the patterns sections, you'll see that patterns are further divided by the type of ribbing. For example, in the "Four-Stitch Patterns" section, there are patterns that work best with K1, P1 ribbing and patterns that work best with P1, K1 ribbing. Using the suggested ribbing for the patterns will create a smooth transition between the cuff and the leg pattern of your socks.

The charts for the stitch patterns represent what the knitting looks like from the right side or outside of the work and are for working the patterns in the round only. All charts are read from right to left for every row and from bottom to top. For example, work the first round by knitting the stitches in the chart from right to left and repeat that sequence until you have completed the first round. Then move to the second row of the chart and begin working those stitches, also from right to left, until that round is complete.

The written directions for the patterns have been edited from knitting back and forth to knitting in the round so that you may follow the text if you are more comfortable with that format.

SYMBOL KEY FOR CHARTS

- K
- P
- K1-b
- No stitch
- sl 1 wyib
- sl 1 wyif
- YO
- 2 Knit into front and then back of the YO
- M M1
- M M1R
- K1, YO, K1 in same st
- K1, P1, K1 in front of same st
- 5 Work 5 sts (K1, YO, K1, YO, K1) into next 2 sts tog
- ssk
- K2tog
- K3tog
- TW2R: K2tog, leave sts on left needle, knit first st and slip both sts off needle
- sl 1, K2tog, psso: slip next st, knit next 2 sts tog, then pass slipped st over 2 sts knit tog

- sl 2, K1, p2sso: insert needle into next 2 sts on left needle as if to K2tog, and slip them to right needle, knit next st, then pass 2 slipped sts tog over knit st
- P2tog
- P3tog
- P3tog, knit same 3 sts tog, purl same 3 sts tog again, and slip all 3 from needle
- K3 and pass first st over next 2 sts
- Knit the third st, purl the second st, knit the first st and let all 3 drop from left needle
- sl 2 sts to cn and hold at front, ssk from left needle, YO, K2 from cn
- sl 3 sts to cn and hold at back, K1 from left needle, sl 2 from cn to left needle, take cn to front, K2 from left needle, K1 from cn
- sl 3 sts to cn and hold at front, K2 from left needle, sl 1 from cn to left needle, take cn to back, K1 from left needle, K2 from cn.

FOUR-STITCH PATTERNS

(Directions begin on page 10.) The written instructions begin with a stitch (indicated in brackets), and the charts begin with a separate column. This extra stitch is worked only once at the beginning of the round of the instep. When working the leg, work only the five-stitch repeats. The extra stitch balances the total pattern on the instep.

PATTERNS FOR K1, P1 RIBBING

Basket Weave

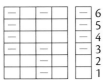

Rnds 1, 2: [K1], *K1, P1, K2, rep from *.
Rnd 3: [P1], *K1, P1, K1, P1, rep from *.
Rnds 4, 5: [P1], *K3, P1, rep from *.
Rnd 6: [P1], *K1, P1, K1, P1, rep from *.
Rep rnds 1–6.

Seeded Ribbing

Rnd 1: [K1], *K1, P1, K2, rep from *.
Rnd 2: [K1], *P3, K1, rep from *.
Rep rnds 1 and 2.

Seeded Ribbing Check

Rnds 1, 3, 5, 7: [K1], *K1, P1, K2, rep from *.
Rnds 2, 4, 6: [K1], *P3, K1, rep from *.
Rnds 8, 10, 12: [P1], *K3, P1, rep from *.
Rnds 9, 11, 13: [P1], *P1, K1, P2, rep from *.
Rnd 14: [P1], *K3, P1, rep from *.
Rep rnds 1–14.

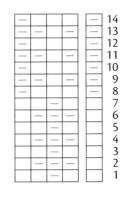

Stansfield 12

Rnds 1, 2: [P1], *K1, P3, rep from *.
Rnds 3, 4: [P1], *K1, P1, K1, P1, rep from *.
Rnds 5, 6: [P1], *P2, K1, P1, rep from *.
Rnds 7, 8: [P1], *K1, P1, K1, P1, rep from *.
Rep rnds 1–8.

Double Basket Weave

Rnds 1, 3, 5, 7: [K1], knit.
Rnds 2, 4: [K1], *P3, K1, rep from *.
Rnds 6, 8: [P1], *P1, K1, P2, rep from *.
Rep rnds 1–8.

Uneven Ribbing

Rnds 1, 3: [K1], *K1, P2, K1, rep from *.

Rnd 2: [K1], *P2, K2, rep from *.

Rnd 4: [K1], *P2, K2, rep from *.

Rep rnds 1–4.

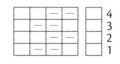

Crossed Ribbing

Rnds 1, 2, 3, 4: [P1], *K1, P1, K1, P1, rep from *.

Rnd 5: [P1], *K the 3rd st, purl the 2nd st, knit the first, and let all 3 drop from LH needle, P1, rep from *.

Rnd 6: [P1], *K1, P1, K1, P1, rep from *.

Rep rnds 1–6.

PATTERNS FOR P1, K1 RIBBING

Decorative Ribbing

Rnd 1: [K1-b], *P3, K1-b, rep from *.

Rnd 2: [K1-b], *P1, K1, P1, K1-b, rep from *.

Rep rnds 1 and 2.

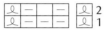

Eyelet Bar

Rnds 1, 3: [K1], *P1, K1-b, P1, K1, rep from *.

Rnd 2: [P1], *P1, K1-b, P2, rep from *.

Rnd 4: [P1], *K3, P1, rep from *.

Rnd 5: [K1], *YO, sl 1, K2tog, psso, YO, K1, rep from *.

Rnd 6: [P1], *K3, P1, rep from *.

Rep rnds 1–6.

Embossed Stitch

Rnds 1, 2, 5, 6: [K1], *P1, K1, P1, K1, rep from *.

Rnds 3, 4: [P1], *K3, P1, rep from *.

Rnds 7, 8: [K1], *K1, P1, K2, rep from *.

Rep rnds 1–8.

Seed-Stitch Ribbing

Rnd 1: [K1], *P1, K1, P1, K1, rep from *.

Rnd 2: [K1], *P3, K1, rep from *.

Rep rnds 1 and 2.

FIVE-STITCH PATTERNS

(Directions begin on page 21.) The written instructions begin with a stitch (indicated in brackets), and the charts begin with a separate column. This extra stitch is worked only once at the beginning of the round of the instep. When working the leg, work only the five-stitch repeats. The extra stitch balances the total pattern on the instep.

PATTERNS FOR P1, K2, P1, K1 RIBBING

Sailor's Ribbing

Rnd 1: [K1-b], *P1, K2, P1, K1-b, rep from *.

Rnd 2: [K1], *P1, K2, P1, K1, rep from *.

Rnd 3: [K1-b], *P4, K1-b, rep from *.

Rnd 4: [K1], *P4, K1, rep from *.

Rep rnds 1–4.

Open Twisted Ribbing

Rnd 1: [K1-b], *P1, K2, P1, K1-b, rep from *.

Rnd 2: [K1-b], *P1, K1, YO, K1, P1, K1-b, rep from *.

Rnd 3: [K1-b], *P1, K3, P1, K1-b, rep from *.

Rnd 4: [K1-b], *P1; K3 and pass first st over next 2 sts; P1, K1-b, rep from *.

Rep rnds 1–4.

Be sure to end with rnd 4 before working next section of sock—the number of stitches changes over the course of the pattern.

Stockinette-Stitch Triangles

Rnd 1: [K1], knit.

Rnd 2: [K1], *P1, K4, rep from *.

Rnd 3: [K1], *P2, K3, rep from *.

Rnd 4: [K1], *P3, K2, rep from *.

Rnd 5: [K1], *P4, K1, rep from *.

Rep rnds 1–5.

Vertical Lace with Twisted Ribbing

Rnd 1: [K1-b], *P1, YO, ssk, P1, K1-b, rep from *.

Rnd 2: [K1-b], *P1, K2, P1, K1-b, rep from *.

Rnd 3: [K1-b], *P1, K2tog, YO, P1, K1-b, rep from *.

Rnd 4: [K1-b], *P1, K2, P1, K1-b, rep from *.

Rep rnds 1–4.

Bell

Rnd 1: [K1-b], *P4, K1-b, rep from *.

Rnd 2: [K1-b], *P2, YO, P2, K1-b, rep from *.

Rnd 3: [K1-b], *P2, [K1, YO, K1, YO, K1, YO, K1] in YO in row below, P2, K1-b, rep from *.

Rnd 4: [K1-b], *P2, K5, K2tog, P2, K1-b, rep from *.

Rnd 5: [K1-b], *P2, K4, K2tog, P2, K1-b, rep from *.

Rnd 6: [K1-b], *P2, K3, K2tog, P2, K1-b, rep from *.

Rnd 7: [K1-b], *P2, K2, K2tog, P2, K1-b, rep from *.

Rnd 8: [K1-b], *P2, K1, K2tog, P2, K1-b, rep from *.

Rnd 9: [K1-b], *P2, K2tog, P2, K1-b, rep from *.

Rnd 10: [K1-b], *P1, P2tog, P2, K1-b, rep from *.

Rep rnds 1–10.

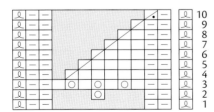

PATTERNS FOR K1, P2, K1, P1 RIBBING

Vertical Eyelets

Rnds 1, 3: [P1], *K4, P1, rep from *.

Rnd 2: [P1], *K1, YO, K2tog, K1, P1, rep from *.

Rnd 4: [P1], *K1, ssk, YO, K1, P1, rep from *.

Rep rnds 1–4.

Ridged Squares

Rnds 1, 3, 5: [K1], knit.

Rnds 2, 4: [P1], *K4, P1, rep from *.

Rnd 6: [P1], purl.

Rep rnds 1–6.

Stansfield 30

Rnd 1: [P1], *P1, K3, P1, rep from *.

Rnd 2: [P1], *K1, P1, K2, P1, rep from *.

Rnd 3: [P1], *K2, P1, K1, P1, rep from *.

Rnd 4: [P1], *K3, P2, rep from *.

Rep rnds 1–4.

Alternating Triangles

Rnd 1: [P1], *K4, P1, rep from *.
Rnd 2: [P1], *K3, P2, rep from *.
Rnd 3: [P1], *K2, P3, rep from *.
Rnd 4: [P1], *K1, P4, rep from *.
Rnd 5: [K1], *P1, K4, rep from *.
Rnd 6: [K1], *P2, K3, rep from *.
Rnd 7: [K1], *P3, K2, rep from *.
Rnd 8: [K1], *P4, K1, rep from *.
Rep rnds 1–8.

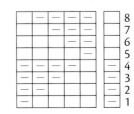

Diagonal Checks

Rnd 1: [P1], *K4, P1, rep from *.

Rnd 2: [P1], *K3, P2, rep from *.

Rnd 3: [P1], *K2, P3, rep from *.

Rnd 4: [P1], *K1, P4, rep from *.

Rnd 5: [K1], *P4, K1, rep from *.

Rnd 6: [K1], *P3, K2, rep from *.

Rnd 7: [K1], *P2, K3, rep from *.

Rnd 8: [K1], *P1, K4, rep from *.

Rep rnds 1–8.

Spindle

Rnds 1, 2, 3, 4: [P1], *K4, P1, rep from *.

Rnds 5, 6, 7, 8: [P1], *P1, K2, P2, rep from *.

Rnds 9, 10: [P1], purl.

Rep rnds 1–10.

SIX-STITCH PATTERNS WITH EVEN INSTEP AND HEEL FLAP

(Directions begin on page 27.) Note that many of the patterns begin and end with P1 so that the patterns will be centered on the instep.

PATTERNS FOR K1, P1 RIBBING

Crosshatch Lace

Rnd 1: *K3, K2tog, YO, K1, rep from *.

Rnd 2: *K2, K2tog, YO, K2, rep from *.

Rnd 3: *K1, K2tog, YO, K3, rep from *.

Rnd 4: *K2tog, YO, K4, rep from *.

Rnd 5: *K1, YO, ssk, K3, rep from *.

Rnd 6: *K2, YO, ssk, K2, rep from *.

Rnd 7: *K3, YO, ssk, K1, rep from *.

Rnd 8: *K4, YO, ssk, rep from *.

Rep rnds 1–8.

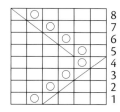

Swedish Block

Rnds 1, 2: *P2, K2, P2, rep from *.

Rnds 3, 4, 5, 6, 7, 8: *K2, P2, K2, rep from *.

Rep rnds 1–8.

Basket Weave

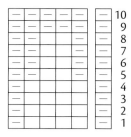

Rnds 1, 6, 7: Knit.

Rnds 2, 3, 4, 5: *K1, P4, K1, rep from *.

Rnds 8, 9, 10, 11: *P2, K2, P2, rep from *.

Rnd 12: Knit.

Rep rnds 1–12.

PATTERNS FOR K1, P1, K2, P1, K1 RIBBING

Double Lace Ribbing

Rnd 1: *K1, P1, YO, ssk, P1, K1, rep from *.

Rnd 2: *K1, P1, K2, P1, K1, rep from *.

Rnd 3: *K1, P1, K2tog, YO, P1, K1, rep from *.

Rnd 4: *K1, P1, K2, P1, K1, rep from *.

Rep rnds 1–4.

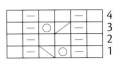

PATTERNS FOR P1, K1, P2, K1, P1 RIBBING

Embossed Moss Stitch

Rnds 1, 2: *P1, K1, P1, K2, P1, rep from *.

Rnds 3, 4: *P1, K2, P1, K1, P1, rep from *.

Rep rnds 1–4.

PATTERNS FOR P1, K4, P1 RIBBING

Broad Spiral Ribbing

Rnds 1, 3: *P1, K4, P1, rep from *.

Rnd 2: *P1, TW2R 2 times, P1, rep from *.

Rnd 4: *P1, K1, TW2R, K1, P1, rep from *.

Rep rnds 1–4.

Italian Chain Ribbing

Rnd 1: *P1, K4, P1, rep from *.

Rnd 2: *P1, K2tog, (YO) twice, ssk, P1, rep from *.

Rnd 3: *P1, K1, P1, K2, P1, rep from *.

Rnd 4: *P1, YO, ssk, K2tog, YO, P1, rep from *.

Rep rnds 1–4.

Faggot and Cable Stripe

Rnds 1, 3, 5, 7, 9, 11: *P1, K2, YO, K2tog, P1, rep from *.

Rnds 2, 4, 6, 8, 10: *P1, ssk, YO, K2, P1, rep from *.

Rnd 12: *P1, sl 2 sts to cn and hold in front, ssk from LH needle, YO, K2 from cn, P1, rep from *.

Rep rnds 1–12.

Vertical Eyelets

Rnd 1: *P1, K1-b, K2, K1-b, P1, rep from *.

Rnds 2, 4: *P1, K4, P1, rep from *.

Rnd 3: *P1, K1-b, YO, K2tog, K1-b, P1, rep from *.

Rnd 5: *P1, K1-b, ssk, YO, K1-b, P1, rep from *.

Rnd 6: *P1, K4, P1, rep from *.

Rep rnds 1–6.

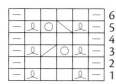

Waving Ribbing

Rnds 1, 2, 3, 4: *P1, K4, P1, rep from *.

Rnds 5, 6, 7, 8: *K2, P2, K2, rep from *.

Rep rnds 1–8.

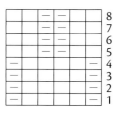

Stansfield 14

Rnds 1, 3: *P1, K4, P1, rep from *.

Rnds 2, 4, 6: Knit.

Rnds 5, 7: *K2, P2, K2, rep from *.

Rnd 8: Knit.

Rep rnds 1–8.

Double Fleck

Rnds 1, 3: Knit.

Rnd 2: *P1, K4, P1, rep from *.

Rnd 4: *K2, P2, K2, rep from *.

Rep rnds 1–4.

Vertical Waffle

Rnds 1, 3, 5, 7, 9: *P1, K4, P1, rep from *.

Rnds 2, 4, 6, 8, 10, 12, 14, 16, 18: Knit.

Rnds 11, 13, 15, 17, 19: *K2, P2, K2, rep from *.

Rnd 20: Knit.

Rep rnds 1–20.

SIX-STITCH PATTERNS WITH UNEVEN INSTEP AND HEEL FLAP

(Directions begin on page 32.) The written instructions begin with a stitch (indicated in brackets), and the charts begin with a separate column. This extra stitch is worked only once at the beginning of the instep round. When working the leg, work only the six-stitch repeats. The extra stitch balances the total pattern on the instep.

PATTERNS FOR K1, P1 RIBBING

Hourglass Eyelets

Rnds 1, 2: [P1], *K5, P1, rep from *.

Rnd 3: [K1], *YO, ssk, P1, K2tog, YO, K1, rep from *.

Rnds 4, 5, 6: [K1], *K2, P1, K3, rep from *.

Rnd 7: [K1], *K2tog, YO, P1, YO, ssk, K1, rep from *.

Rnd 8: [P1], *K5, P1, rep from *.

Rep rnds 1–8.

Shirred Ribbing

Rnds 1, 2: [P1], *K5, P1, rep from *.

Rnd 3: [P1], *M1, K1, P3tog, K1, M1R, P1, rep from *.

Rnd 4: [P1], *K5, P1, rep from *.

Rep rnds 1–4.

Parachute

Rnds 1, 3, 5, 7: [P1], *K5, P1, rep from *.

Rnd 2: [P1], *K2, YO, ssk, K1, P1, rep from *.

Rnd 4: [P1], *K2, YO, K2tog, K1, P1, rep from *.

Rnd 6: [P1], *YO, K1, sl 1, K2tog, psso, K1, YO, P1, rep from *.

Rnd 8: [P1], *K1, YO, sl 1, K2tog, psso, YO, K1, P1, rep from *.

Rep rnds 1–8.

Woven Cable

Rnds 1, 3, 5, 7, 9: [P1], *K5, P1, rep from *.

Rnds 2, 4, 6, 8: [P1], *ssk, YO, K1-b, YO, K2tog, P1, rep from *.

Rnd 10: [P1], *Sl 3 sts to cn and hold in front, K2 from LH needle, sl 1 from cn to LH needle and take cn to back, K1 from LH needle, then K2 from cn, P1.

Rep rnds 1–10.

Little Arrowhead Lace

Rnd 1: [K1-b], *YO, ssk, K1, K2tog, YO, K1-b, rep from *.

Rnd 2: [K1], knit.

Rnd 3: [K1-b], *K1, YO, sl 1, K2tog, psso, YO, K1, K1-b, rep from *.

Rnd 4: [K1], knit.

Rep rnds 1–4.

Lattice Stitch

Rnd 1: [K1], *K2, P1, K3, rep from *.

Rnd 2: [K1], *K1, P1, K1, P1, K2, rep from *.

Rnds 3, 5: [K1], *P1, K3, P1, K1, rep from *.

Rnd 4: [P1], *K5, P1, rep from *.

Rnd 6: [K1], *K1, P1, K1, P1, K2, rep from *.

Rep rnds 1–6.

		–		–			–		6
	–				–				5
–							–		4
		–							3
			–		–				2
				–					1

Cloverleaf Eyelet

Rnds 1, 3, 5: [P1], *K5, P1, rep from *.

Rnd 2: [P1], *K1, YO, sl 1, K2tog, psso, YO, K1, P1, rep from *.

Rnd 4: [P1], *K2, YO, ssk, K1, P1, rep from *.

Rnd 6: [P1], *K5, P1, rep from *.

Rep rnds 1–6.

Reverse Stockinette-Stitch Chevrons

Rnd 1: [P1], *K5, P1, rep from *.

Rnd 2: [P1], *P1, K3, P2, rep from *.

Rnd 3: [K1], *(P2, K1) twice, rep from *.

Rnd 4: [K1], *K1, P3, K2, rep from *.

Rnd 5: [K1], *K2, P1, K3, rep from *.

Rnd 6: [K1], knit.

Rep rnds 1–6.

Stems

Rnds 1, 2: [P1], *K5, P1, rep from *.

Rnd 3: [P1], *K2tog, YO, K1-b, YO, ssk, P1, rep from *.

Rnd 4: [P1], *K5, P1, rep from *.

Rep rnds 1–4.

PATTERNS FOR P1, K1 RIBBING

Small Tiles

Rnd 1: [K1], *P1, K3, P1, K1, rep from *.

Rnd 2: [P1], *P1, K3, P2, rep from *.

Rnd 3: [K1], *P5, K1, rep from *.

Rnd 4: [P1], purl.

Rep rnds 1–4.

Pennant Stitch

Rnd 1: [K1], *P1, K5, rep from *.

Rnd 2: [K1], *P2, K4, rep from *.

Rnds 3, 7: [K1], *P3, K3, rep from *.

Rnds 4, 6: [K1], *P4, K2, rep from *.

Rnd 5: [K1], *P5, K1, rep from *.

Rnd 8: [K1], *P2, K4, rep from *.

Rep rnds 1–8.

EIGHT-STITCH PATTERNS

(Directions begin on page 37.) These patterns are balanced and do not require an extra stitch on the instep. Be careful when working those rounds with a final YO so it does not slip off the needle.

PATTERNS FOR K1, P1 RIBBING

Traveling Vine

Rnd 1: *YO, K1-b, YO, ssk, K5, rep from *.

Rnd 2: *K3, ssk, K4, rep from *.

Rnd 3: *YO, K1-b, YO, K2, ssk, K3, rep from *.

Rnd 4: *K5, ssk, K2, rep from *.

Rnd 5: *K1-b, YO, K4, ssk, K1, YO, rep from *.

Rnd 6: *K6, ssk, K1, rep from *.

Rnd 7: *K5, K2tog, YO, K1-b, YO, rep from *.

Rnd 8: *K4, K2tog, K3, rep from *.

Rnd 9: *K3, K2tog, K2, YO, K1-b, YO, rep from *.

Rnd 10: *K3, K2tog, K4, rep from *.

Rnd 11: *YO, K1, K2tog, K4, YO, K1-b, rep from *.

Rnd 12: *K1, K2tog, K6, rep from *.

Rep rnds 1–12.

Scrolls

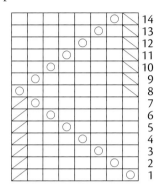

Rnd 1: *YO, K6, K2tog, rep from *.

Rnd 2: *K1, YO, K5, K2tog, rep from *.

Rnd 3: *K2, YO, K4, K2tog, rep from *.

Rnd 4: *K3, YO, K3, K2tog, rep from *.

Rnd 5: *K4, YO, K2, K2tog, rep from *.

Rnd 6: *K5, YO, K1, K2tog, rep from *.

Rnd 7: *K6, YO, K2tog, rep from *.

Rnd 8: *Ssk, K6, YO, rep from *.

Rnd 9: *Ssk, K5, YO, K1, rep from *.

Rnd 10: *Ssk, K4, YO, K2, rep from *.

Rnd 11: *Ssk, K3, YO, K3, rep from *.

Rnd 12: *Ssk, K2, YO, K4, rep from *.

Rnd 13: *Ssk, K1, YO, K5, rep from *.

Rnd 14: *Ssk, YO, K6, rep from *.

Rep rnds 1–14.

Stansfield 16

Rnds 1, 2: *K1, P6, K1, rep from *.

Rnd 3: Knit.

Rnds 4, 5: *P3, K2, P3, rep from *.

Rnd 6: Knit.

Rep rnds 1–6.

Grapevine

Rnds 1, 3, 5, 7, 9, 11: Knit.

Rnd 2: *K2tog, K1, YO, K1, ssk, K2, rep from *.

Rnd 4: *YO, K1, YO, K1, ssk, K2tog, K1, rep from *.

Rnd 6: *YO, K3, YO, K1, ssk, K1, rep from *.

Rnd 8: *K2, K2tog, K1, YO, K1, ssk, rep from *.

Rnd 10: *Ssk, K2tog, (K1, YO) twice, K1, rep from *.

Rnd 12: *K1, K2tog, K1, YO, K3, YO, rep from *.

Rep rnds 1–12.

Pennants

Rnds 1, 7: *K3, P1, K1, P3, rep from *.

Rnds 2, 6: *(K2, P2) twice, rep from *.

Rnds 3, 5: *K1, P3, K3, P1, rep from *.

Rnd 4: *P4, K4, rep from *.

Rnd 8: *K4, P4, rep from *.

Rep rnds 1–8.

PATTERNS FOR P1, K2, P2, K2, P1 RIBBING

Milanese Lace

Rnd 1: *P1, K4, K2tog, YO, P1, rep from *.

Rnd 2: *P1, K3, K2tog, K1, YO, P1, rep from *.

Rnd 3: *P1, K2, K2tog, K2, YO, P1, rep from *.

Rnd 4: *P1, K1, K2tog, K3, YO, P1, rep from *.

Rnd 5: *P1, K2tog, K4, YO, P1, rep from *.

Rnd 6: *P1, YO, K4, K2tog, P1, rep from *.

Rnd 7: *P1, K1, YO, K3, K2tog, P1, rep from *.

Rnd 8: *P1, K2, YO, K2, K2tog, P1, rep from *.

Rnd 9: *P1, K3, YO, K1, K2tog, P1, rep from *.

Rnd 10: *P1, K4, YO, K2tog, P1, rep from *.

Rep rnds 1–10.

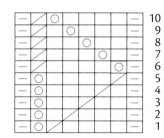

Stansfield 196

Rnds 1, 2, 4, 6, 8, 9, 10, 12, 14: *P1, K6, P1, rep from *.

Rnd 3: *P1, YO, K2, ssk, K2, P1, rep from *.

Rnd 5: *P1, K1, YO, K2, ssk, K1, P1, rep from *.

Rnd 7: *P1, K2, YO, K2, ssk, P1, rep from *.

Rnd 11: *P1, K2, K2tog, K2, YO, P1, rep from *.

Rnd 13: *P1, K1, K2tog, K2, YO, K1, P1, rep from *.

Rnd 15: *P1, K2tog, K2, YO, K2, P1, rep from *.

Rnd 16: *P1, K6, P1, rep from *.

Rep rnds 1–16.

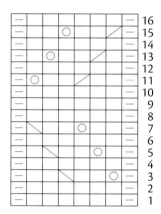

Cross-Stitch Block

Rnds 1, 3, 5, 7: Knit.

Rnds 2, 4, 6, 8: *K3, P2, K3, rep from *.

Rnds 9, 11: *K2, (sl 1 wyib, K2) twice, rep from *.

Rnds 10, 12: *P2, (sl 1 wyib, P2) twice, rep from *.

Rnd 13: *K2, sl 3 wyib to cn and hold in back, knit next st, sl 2 from cn to LH needle and bring cn with 1 st to front, K2 from LH needle, K1 from cn, K2, rep from *.

Rnd 14: *K3, P2, K3, rep from *.

Rep rnds 1–14.

TEN-STITCH PATTERNS

(Directions begin on page 42.) The written instructions begin with a stitch (indicated in brackets), and the charts begin with a separate column. This extra stitch is worked only once at the beginning of the round of the instep. When working the leg, work only the 10-stitch repeats. The extra stitch balances the total pattern on the instep.

PATTERNS FOR P1, K1 RIBBING

Spaced Checks

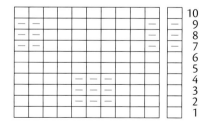

Rnds 1, 5, 6: [K1], knit.

Rnds 2, 3, 4: [K1], *K3, P3, K4, rep from *.

Rnds 7, 8, 9: [P1], *P1, K7, P2, rep from *.

Rnd 10: [K1], knit.

Rep rnds 1–10.

Leafy Lace

Rnds 1, 3: [K1-b], *P9, K1-b, rep from *.

Rnds 2, 4: [K1], *P9, K1, rep from *.

Rnd 5: [K1-b], *P2, P2tog, YO, K1-b, YO, P2tog, P2, K1-b, rep from *.

Rnd 6: [K1], *P4, K1-b, P4, K1, rep from *.

Rnd 7: [K1-b], *P1, P2tog, YO, K1-b 3 times, YO, P2tog, P1, K1-b, rep from *.

Rnds 8, 14: [K1], *P3, K1-b 3 times, P3, K1, rep from *.

Rnd 9: [K1-b], *P2tog, YO, K1-b 5 times, YO, P2tog, K1-b, rep from *.

Rnds 10, 12: [K1], *P2, K1-b 5 times, P2, K1, rep from *.

Rnd 11: [K1-b], *P1, YO, K1-b twice, sl 2 tog kw, K1, P2sso, K1-b twice, YO, P1, K1-b, rep from *.

Rnd 13: [K1-b], *P2, YO, K1-b, sl 2 tog kw, K1, P2sso, K1-b, YO, P2, K1-b, rep from *.

Rnd 15: [K1-b], P3, YO, sl 2 tog kw, K1, P2sso, YO, P3, K1-b, rep from *.

Rnd 16: [K1], *P4, K1-b, P4, K1, rep from *.

Rep rnds 1–16.

Waffle Stitch

Rnds 1, 2, 3: [K1], *P3, K3, P3, K1, rep from *.

Rnd 4: [P1], purl.

Rep rnds 1–4.

PATTERNS FOR K1, P1 RIBBING

Garter Ribbing

Rnds 1, 3: [K1], *P1, K7, P1, K1, rep from *.

Rnds 2, 4: [K1], *P1, K1, P5, K1, P1, K1, rep from *.

Rnds 5, 7: [K1], *K3, P1, K1, P1, K4, rep from *.

Rnds 6, 8: [P1], *P2, (K1, P1) twice, K1, P3, rep from *.

Rep rnds 1–8.

Moss Diamonds

Rnds 1, 2, 9, 10: [P1], *K3, P1, K1, P1, K3, P1, rep from *.

Rnds 3, 4, 7, 8: [K1], *(P1, K3) twice, P1, K1, rep from *.

Rnds 5, 6: [P1], *K1, P1, (K2, P1) twice, K1, P1, rep from *.

Rnds 11, 12: [P1], *K2, (P1, K1) 3 times, K1, P1, rep from *.

Rep rnds 1–12.

Fan Lace

Rnd 1: [P1], purl.

Rnd 2: [P1], *YO, K3, sl 2 tog kw, K1, p2sso, K3, YO, P1, rep from *.

Rnd 3: [P1], *K9, P1, rep from *.

Rnd 4: [P1], *P1, YO, K2, sl 2 tog kw, K1, p2sso, K2, YO, P2, rep from *.

Rnd 5: [P1], *P1, K7, P2, rep from *.

Rnd 6: [P1], *P2, YO, K1, sl 2 tog kw, K1, p2sso, K1, YO, P3, rep from *.

Rnd 7: [P1], *P2, K5, P3, rep from *.

Rnd 8: [P1], *P3, YO, sl 2 tog kw, K1, p2sso, YO, P4, rep from *.

Rep rnds 1–8.

Eyelets and Waves

Rnds 1, 3, 5: [K1-b], *YO, K2, K2tog, K1, ssk, K2, YO, K1-b, rep from *.

Rnds 2, 4, 6, 8, 10, 12: [K1], knit.

Rnd 7: [K1], *K1, YO, K2, sl 2 tog kw, K1, p2sso, K2, YO, K2, rep from *.

Rnd 9: [K1], *K2, YO, K1, sl 2 tog kw, K1, p2sso, K1, YO, K3, rep from *.

Rnd 11: [K1], *K3, YO, sl 2 tog kw, K1, p2sso, YO, K4, rep from *.

Rnds 13, 14: [P1], purl.

Rep rnds 1–14.

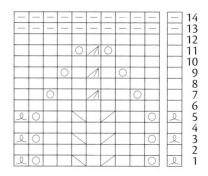

Mosaic

Rnds 1, 2, 3, 4: [K1], *P3, K1, P1, K1, P3, K1, rep from *.

Rnds 5, 6, 7, 8: [P1], *K1, P3, K1, P3, K1, P1, rep from *.

Rep rnds 1–8.

Little Chevron Ribbing

Rnd 1: [P1], *K1, P1, (K2, P1) twice, K1, P1, rep from *.

Rnd 2: [P1], *K2, (P1, K1) twice, P1, K2, P1, rep from *.

Rnd 3: [P1], *K3, P3, K3, P1, rep from *.

Rnd 4: [P1], *(P1, K3) twice, P2, rep from *.

Rep rnds 1–4.

Embossed Diamonds

Rnds 1, 7: [K1], *(P1, K3) twice, P1, K1, rep from *.

Rnds 2, 6: [P1], *K3, P1, K1, P1, K3, P1, rep from *.

Rnds 3, 5: [K1], *K2, (P1, K1) 3 times, K2, rep from *.

Rnd 4: [K1], *(K1, P1) 4 times, K2, rep from *.

Rnd 8: [P1], *K1, P1, K5, P1, K1, P1, rep from *.

Rnd 9: [K1], *(P1, K1) twice, K2, (P1, K1) twice, rep from *.

Rnd 10: [P1], *K1, P1, K5, P1, K1, P1, rep from *.

Rep rnds 1–10.

Stansfield 27

Rnds 1, 3, 5, 7, 9: [K1], *K1, P7, K2, rep from *.

Rnds 2, 4, 6, 8, 10, 12: [K1], knit.

Rnds 11, 13: [P1], *P1, K7, P2, rep from *.

Rnd 14: [K1], knit.

Rep rnds 1–14.

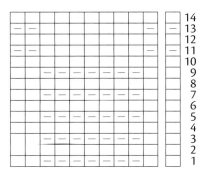

TWELVE-STITCH PATTERNS

(Directions begin on page 47.) The written instructions begin with a stitch (indicated in brackets), and the charts begin with a separate column. This extra stitch is worked only once at the beginning of the instep round. When working the leg, work only the 12-stitch repeats. The extra stitch balances the total pattern on the instep.

PATTERNS FOR K1, P1 RIBBING

Crest of the Wave

Rnds 1, 3, 6, 8, 10: [K1], knit.

Rnds 2, 4: [P1], purl.

Rnds 5, 7, 9, 11: [K1], *K2tog twice, (YO, K1) 3 times, YO, ssk twice, K1, rep from *.

Rnd 12: [K1], knit.

Rep rnds 1–12.

Stansfield 26

Rnds 1, 2, 5, 6, 9, 10, 13, 14: [K1], knit.

Rnds 3, 4, 7, 8: [K1], *K2, P7, K3, rep from *.

Rnds 11, 12, 15, 16: [P1], *P3, K5, P4, rep from *.

Rep rnds 1–16.

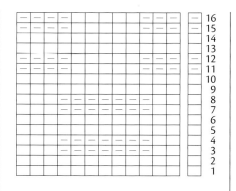

Baby Fern

Rnds 1, 3, 5: [K1], knit.

Rnd 2: [K1], *P1, K2tog, K2, YO, K1, YO, K2, ssk, P1, K1, rep from *.

Rnd 4: [K1], *P1, K2tog, K1, YO, K3, YO, K1, ssk, P1, K1, rep from *.

Rnd 6: [K1], *P1, K2tog, YO, K5, YO, ssk, P1, K1, rep from *.

Rep rnds 1–6.

Stansfield 304

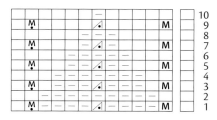

Rnd 1: [K1], *M1, P4, P3tog, P4, M1R, K1, rep from *.

Rnd 2: [K1], *K1, P9, K2, rep from *.

Rnd 3: [K1], *M1, K1, P3, P3tog, P3, K1, M1R, K1, rep from *.

Rnd 4: [K1], *K2, P7, K3, rep from *.

Rnd 5: [K1], *M1, K2, P2, P3tog, P2, K2, M1R, K1, rep from *.

Rnd 6: [K1], *K3, P5, K4, rep from *.

Rnd 7: [K1], *M1, K3, P1, P3tog, P1, K3, M1R, K1, rep from *.

Rnd 8: [K1], *K4, P3, K5, rep from *.

Rnd 9: [K1], *M1, K4, P3tog, K4, M1R, K1, rep from *.

Rnd 10: [K1], *K5, P1, K6, rep from *.

Rep rnds 1–10.

King Charles Brocade

Rnd 1: [K1], *P1, K9, P1, K1, rep from *.

Rnd 2: [P1], *K1, P1, K7, P1, K1, P1, rep from *.

Rnds 3, 11: [K1], *P1, K1, P1, K5, (P1, K1) twice, rep from *.

Rnds 4, 10: [K1], *(K1, P1) twice, K3, (P1, K1) twice, K1, rep from *.

Rnds 5, 9: [K1], *K2, (P1, K1) 4 times, K2, rep from *.

Rnds 6, 8: [K1], *K3, (P1, K1) 3 times, K3, rep from *.

Rnd 7: [K1], *K4, (P1, K1) twice, K4, rep from *.

Rnd 12: [P1], ^K1, P1, K7, P1, K1, P1, rep from *.

Rep rnds 1–12.

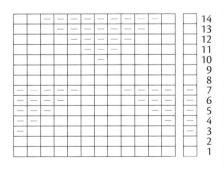

Triangles

Rnds 1, 2, 8, 9: [K1], knit.

Rnd 3: [P1], *K11, P1, rep from *.

Rnd 4: [P1], *P1, K9, P2, rep from *.

Rnd 5: [P1], *P2, K7, P3, rep from *.

Rnd 6: [P1], *P3, K5, P4, rep from *.

Rnd 7: [P1], *P4, K3, P5, rep from *.

Rnd 10: [K1], *K5, P1, K6, rep from *.

Rnd 11: [K1], *K4, P3, K5, rep from *.

Rnd 12: [K1], *K3, P5, K4, rep from *.

Rnd 13: [K1], *K2, P7, K3, rep from *.

Rnd 14: [K1], *K1, P9, K2, rep from *.

Rep rnds 1–14.

PATTERNS FOR P1, K1 RIBBING

Leaf Ribbing

Rnds 1, 2: [K1], *P1, K1, (P3, K1) twice, P1, K1, rep from *.

Rnds 3, 4: [K1], *P1, K2, P2, K1, P2, K2, P1, K1, rep from *.

Rnds 5, 6: [K1], *P1, K3, P1, K1, P1, K3, P1, K1, rep from *.

Rnds 7, 8: [K1], *P2, K2, P1, K1, P1, K2, P2, K1, rep from *.

Rnds 9, 10: [K1], *P3, (K1, P1) twice, K1, P3, K1, rep from *.

Rep rnds 1–10.

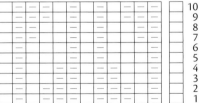

Fern Stitch

Rnd 1: [K1-b], *P4, K3, P4, K1-b, rep from *.

Rnd 2: [K1], *P4, K3, P4, K1, rep from *.

Rnd 3: [K1-b], *P3, K2tog, (K1, YO, K1 into next st), ssk, P3, K1-b, rep from *.

Rnd 4: [K1], *P3, K5, P3, K1, rep from *.

Rnd 5: [K1-b], *P2, K2tog, K1, (K1, YO, K1 into next st), K1, ssk, P2, K1-b, rep from *.

Rnd 6: [K1], *P2, K7, P2, K1, rep from *.

Rnd 7: [K1-b], *P1, K2tog, K2, (K1, YO, K1 into next st), K2, ssk, P1, K1-b, rep from *.

Rnd 8: [K1], *P1, K9, P1, K1, rep from *.

Rnd 9: [K1-b], *K2tog, K3, (K1, YO, K1 into next st), K3, ssk, K1-b, rep from *.

Rnd 10: [K1], knit.

Rep rnds 1–10.

SIX-STITCH STRANDED PATTERNS

(Directions begin on page 52.) Work the leg pattern for as many repeats as you need for the desired leg length. For balance, you may want to work the first few rows of the leg pattern at the ankle to create symmetry on the leg. For a complementary look, the sole pattern repeats a design element from the leg pattern.

Arches (Leg Pattern)

Arches (Sole Pattern)

Hourglass (Leg Pattern)

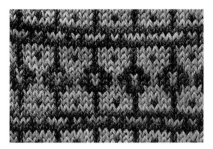

Hourglass (Sole Pattern)

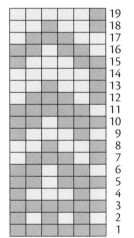

Diamonds (Leg Pattern)

10
9
8
7
6
5
4
3
2
1

Diamonds (Sole Pattern)

5
4
3
2
1

Moorish Stripe (Leg Pattern)

13
12
11
10
9
8
7
6
5
4
3
2
1

Moorish Stripe (Sole Pattern)

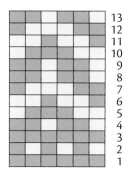

6
5
4
3
2
1

Blocks (Leg Pattern)

8
7
6
5
4
3
2
1

Blocks (Sole Pattern)

8
7
6
5
4
3
2
1

Enclosed Stars
(Leg Pattern)

16
15
14
13
12
11
10
9
8
7
6
5
4
3
2
1

Enclosed Stars
(Sole Pattern)

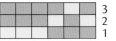

3
2
1

SIX-STITCH TESSELLATED PATTERNS

(Directions begin on page 57.) These patterns are fun to knit and you can use as few or as many colors as you like to work them. You need to choose a leg pattern, an instep pattern, and a sole pattern from those presented here, or use some graph paper and make one yourself.

LEG PATTERNS
Faux Entrelac

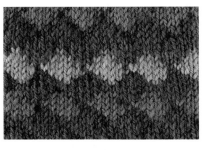

30
29
28
27
26
25
24
23
22
21
20
19
18
17
16
15
14
13
12
11
10
9
8
7
6
5
4
3
2
1

Waves

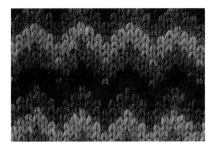

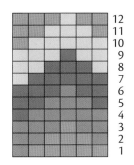

12
11
10
9
8
7
6
5
4
3
2
1

Heart Crook

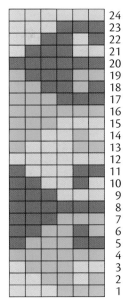

24
23
22
21
20
19
18
17
16
15
14
13
12
11
10
9
8
7
6
5
4
3
2
1

Komi Vine

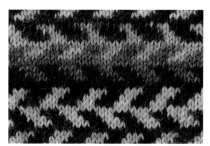

40
39
38
37
36
35
34
33
32
31
30
29
28
27
26
25
24
23
22
21
20
19
18
17
16
15
14
13
12
11
10
9
8
7
6
5
4
3
2
1

Heart

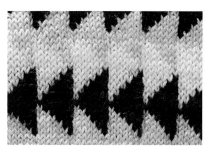

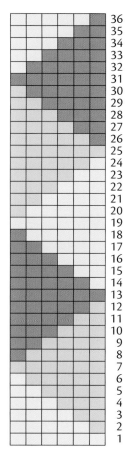

36
35
34
33
32
31
30
29
28
27
26
25
24
23
22
21
20
19
18
17
16
15
14
13
12
11
10
9
8
7
6
5
4
3
2
1

Swedish Block

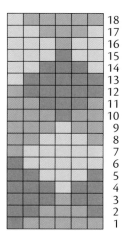

18
17
16
15
14
13
12
11
10
9
8
7
6
5
4
3
2
1

INSTEP PATTERNS

Komi Star (Instep 1)

6
5
4
3
2
1

Instep 2

```
6
5
4
3
2
1
```

Instep 3

```
14
13
12
11
10
9
8
7
6
5
4
3
2
1
```

Instep 4

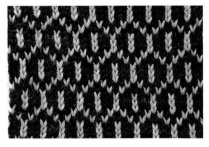

```
10
9
8
7
6
5
4
3
2
1
```

Instep 5

```
8
7
6
5
4
3
2
1
```

Instep 6

SOLE PATTERNS

Pinstripe

```
1
```

Checkerboard

```
2
1
```

Lice

```
2
1
```

TEN-STITCH MOSAIC PATTERNS

(Directions begin on page 62.) On the right-hand side of each chart is a column of white and black squares separated by a blank column. Refer to this first column of squares when working the charts. The basic rule is that on all rows that begin with a white square, you work white squares and slip the black squares. On all rows that begin with a black square, you work the black squares and slip the white squares. Work all even-numbered rows as indicated in the text. On all rounds, work all slipped stitches by slipping purlwise with the yarn in back.

On the even-numbered rounds, you have the choice of knitting or purling the rounds. If you purl the rounds, it will create a garter-stitch fabric, and if you knit, it will yield a stockinette fabric. All the swatch samples were knit as garter-stitch fabric—purl on the even-numbered rows, yielding a more textured fabric.

Simulated Basket Weave

Rnd 1: With light, *K1, sl 1, K6, sl 1, K1, rep from *.

Rnd 2 and all even-numbered rnds: With same color as previous rnd, knit (or purl) same sts worked on previous rnd; sl same slipped sts.

Rnds 3, 15: With dark, *sl 1, K8, sl 1, rep from *.

Rnds 5, 13: With light, *(K1, sl 1) twice, K2, (sl 1, K1) twice, rep from *.

Rnds 7, 11: With dark, *K4, sl 2, K4, rep from *.

Rnd 9: With light, *K3, sl 1, K2, sl 1, K3, rep from *.

Rnd 16: As rnd 2.

Rep rnds 1–16.

T Pattern

Rnd 1: With light, *sl 1, K8, sl 1, rep from *.

Rnd 2 and all even-numbered rnds: With same color as previous rnd, knit (or purl) same sts worked on previous rnd; sl same slipped sts.

Rnd 3: With dark, *K1, sl 1, K6, sl 1, K1, rep from *.

Rnd 5: With light, *K4, sl 2, K4, rep from *.

Rnd 7: With dark, *K3, sl 1, K2, sl 1, K3, rep from *.

Rnd 8: As rnd 2.

Rep rnds 1–8.

Chevron

Rnd 1: With light, knit.

Rnd 2 and all even-numbered rnds: With same color as previous rnd, knit (or purl) same sts worked on previous rnd; sl same slipped sts.

Rnd 3: With dark, *(K1, sl 1) 4 times, K2, rep from *.

Rnd 5: With light, *sl 1, K7, sl 1, K1, rep from *.

Rnd 7: With dark, *K2, sl 1, (K1, sl 1) twice, K3, rep from *.

Rnd 9: With light, *K1, sl 1, K5, sl 1, K1, sl 1, rep from *.

Rnd 11: With dark, *K3, sl 1, K1, sl 1, K4, rep from *.

Rnd 13: With light, *(sl 1, K1) twice, K2, (sl 1, K1) twice, rep from *.

Rnd 15: With dark, knit.

Rnd 17: With light, *(K1, sl 1) 4 times, K2, rep from *.

Rnd 19: With dark, *sl 1, K7, sl 1, K1, rep from *.

Rnd 21: With light, *K2, (sl 1, K1) 3 times, K2, rep from *.

Rnd 23: With dark, *K1, sl 1, K5, sl 1, K1, sl 1, rep from *.

Rnd 25: With light, *K3, (sl 1, K1) twice, K3, rep from *.

Rnd 27: With dark, *sl 1, K1, sl 1, K3, (sl 1, K1) twice, rep from *.

Rnd 28: As rnd 2.

Rep rnds 1–28.

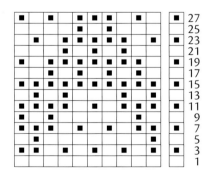

Diamond

Rnd 1: With light, *sl 1, K9, rep from *.

Rnd 2 and all even-numbered rnds: With same color as previous rnd, knit (or purl) same sts worked on previous rnd; sl same slipped sts.

Rnds 3, 23: With dark, *K2, (sl 1, K1) 4 times, rep from *.

Rnds 5, 21: With light, *K1, sl 1, K7, sl 1, rep from *.

Rnds 7, 19: With dark, *K3, (sl 1, K1) 3 times, K1, rep from *.

Rnds 9, 17: With light, *(sl 1, K1) 2 times, K4, sl 1, K1, rep from *.

Rnds 11, 15: With dark, *K4, sl 1, K1, sl 1, K3, rep from *.

Rnd 13: With light, *(K1, sl 1) twice, K2, (K1, sl 1) twice, rep from *.

Rnd 24: As rnd 2.

Rep rnds 1–24.

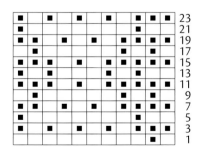

Stepped Fret

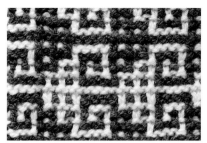

Rnd 1: With light, knit.

Rnd 2 and all even-numbered rnds: With same color as previous rnd, knit (or purl) same sts worked on previous rnd; sl same slipped sts.

Rnds 3, 27: With dark, *(sl 1, K1) 3 times, K4, rep from *.

Rnds 5, 25: With light, *K5, sl 1, K3, sl 1, rep from *.

Rnds 7, 23: With dark, *(sl 1, K1) twice, K2, (sl 1, K1) twice, rep from *.

Rnds 9, 21: With light, *K2, (K1, sl 1) 4 times, rep from *.

Rnds 11, 19: With dark, *sl 1, K5, sl 1, K3, rep from *.

Rnds 13, 17: With light, *(K1, sl 1) 3 times, K4, rep from *.

Rnd 15: With dark, knit.

Rnd 28: As rnd 2.

Rep rnds 1–28.

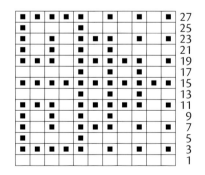

Syncopation

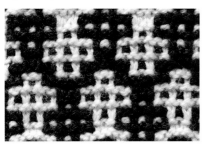

Rnd 1: With light, *K4, sl 3, K3, rep from *.

Rnd 2 and all even-numbered rnds: With same color as previous rnd, knit (or purl) same sts worked on previous rnd; sl same slipped sts.

Rnd 3: With dark, *(K1, sl 1) twice, K3, sl 1, K1, sl 1, rep from *.

Rnds 5, 13: With light, *K4, sl 1, K1, sl 1, K3, rep from *.

Rnds 7, 35: With dark, *K1, sl 1, K7, sl 1, rep from *.

Rnd 9: With light, *K2, (sl 1, K1) 4 times, rep from *.

Rnd 11: With dark, *sl 2, K7, sl 1, rep from *.

Rnd 15: With dark, *K2, sl 2, K3, sl 2, K1, rep from *.

Rnds 17, 25: With light, *K1, sl 1, K7, sl 1, rep from *.

Rnd 19: With dark, *K4, sl 3, K3, rep from *.

Rnd 21: With light, *(K1, sl 1) twice, K2, (K1, sl 1) twice, rep from *.

Rnds 23, 31: With dark, *K4, sl 1, K1, sl 1, K3, rep from *.

Rnd 27: With dark, *K2, (sl 1, K1) 4 times, rep from *.

Rnd 29: With light, *sl 2, K7, sl 1, rep from *.

Rnd 33: With light, *K2, sl 2, K3, sl 2, K1, rep from *.

Rnd 36: As rnd 2.

Rep rnds 1–36.

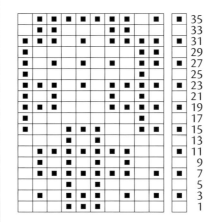

Curled Cross

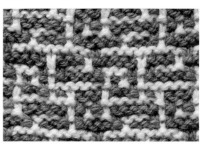

Rnd 1: With light, *K2, (sl 1, K1) twice, K4, rep from *.

Rnd 2 and all even-numbered rnds: With same color as previous rnd, knit (or purl) same sts worked on previous rnd; sl same slipped sts.

Rnd 3: With dark, *(K1, sl 1) 3 times, K4, rep from *.

Rnd 5: With light, *(sl 1, K1) twice, K2, sl 1, K3, rep from *.

Rnd 7: With dark, *K1, sl 1, K5, sl 1, K2, rep from *.

Rnd 9: With light, *K6, sl 1, K3, rep from *.

Rnd 11: With dark, *K3, sl 1, K5, sl 1, rep from *.

Rnd 13: With light, *(sl 1, K3) twice, sl 1, K1, rep from *.

Rnd 15: With dark, *K5, (sl 1, K1) twice, sl 1, rep from *.

Rnd 17: With light, *K6, (sl 1, K1) twice, rep from *.

Rnd 19: With dark, *K1, sl 1, (K3, sl 1) twice, rep from *.

Rnd 20: As rnd 2.

Rep rnds 1–20.

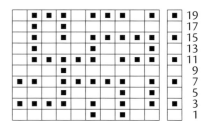

RESOURCES

For a list of shops in your area that carry the yarns used in this book, contact the following companies.

Briggs & Little Woolen Mills, Ltd.
Harvey, York Co.
New Brunswick, Canada E6K 1J8
800-561-9276
Tuffy and Durasport

Candace Strick
www.strickwear.com
Fingering weight

Dale of Norway Yarn
www.daleyarns.com
Baby Ull

French Hill Farm
Bill and Diane Trussell
PO Box 82
Solon, ME 04979
207-643-2540
Coopworth roving (yarn hand spun by the author)

Knit Picks
www.knitpicks.com
Essential

Lana Grossa
Unicorn Books and Crafts, Inc.
www.unicornbooks.com
Meilenweit 6 fach

Lisa Souza Knitwear and Dyeworks
lisa@lisaknit.com
www.lisaknit.com
Sock!

Lorna's Laces
www.lornaslaces.net
Shepherd Sport
Shepherd Worsted

Louet Sales
www.louet.com
Gems Merino Opal

Mountain Colors
www.mountaincolors.com
Weaver's Wool Quarters
Bearfoot

Schaefer Yarn Company
www.schaeferyarn.com
Lola

Simply Socks Yarn Company
www.simplysockyarn.com
Lang Jawoll Superwash

Tricia and Chet Petkiewicz
T & C Imports
tandcimports@comcast.net
Alpaca
Frog Tree

Twist of Fate Spinnery
TwistofFatespinnery@hotmail.com
South Down Sock

ABOUT THE AUTHOR

Charlene Schurch is the author of several books and numerous articles about knitting. Her articles have appeared in *Piecework, Spin-Off, Vogue Knitting, Interweave Knits,* and *Knitter's Magazine.* Charlene teaches knitting and dyeing nationally and lives in Florida and Connecticut with her husband, Fred, and cat, Lucy.

INDEX